Language:
The Basics

What makes human language unique?
Do women speak differently from men?
Just what is the meaning of 'meaning'?
Are some forms of English better than others?
What do linguists actually do?

Language: The Basics is not a textbook; it does not attempt to provide a comprehensive introduction to the subject. Instead it gently introduces beginning students and general readers to the study of language. Written in an engaging and entertaining style, this book provides an overview of the key topics and an explanation of the basic terms and ideas.

Language: The Basics encourages the reader to think about the way language works and look again at some popular misconceptions about language and what linguists do. An ideal book for all school, college and university students and an essential purchase for anyone who's been accused of splitting an infinitive.

R.L. Trask is currently lecturer in linguistics at the University of Sussex and author of *A Dictionary of Grammatical Terms in Linguistics* and *Language Change*.

Other titles in this series include:

Philosophy: The Basics
Nigel Warburton

Politics: The Basics
Steven D. Tansey

LONDON AND NEW YORK

Language:
The Basics

R.L. Trask

First published 1995
by Routledge
11 New Fetter Lane,
London EC4P 4EE

Simultaneously published in the
USA and Canada
by Routledge
29 West 35th Street, New York,
NY 10001

© 1995 R.L. Trask

Typeset in Times by
Solidus (Bristol) Limited
Printed and bound in Great Britain
by TJ Press (Padstow) Ltd,
Padstow, Cornwall

*British Library Cataloguing in
Publication Data*
A catalogue record for this book is
available from the British Library

*Library of Congress Cataloguing
in Publication Data*
A catalogue record for this book
has been requested

ISBN 0–415–12540–5 (hbk)
ISBN 0–415–12541–3 (pbk)

*To my mother
and
to the memory of my father*

Contents

Contents

Illustrations

Illustrations

To the reader

The book in your hand is not a textbook: it makes no attempt at comprehensive coverage, and it contains no exercises. Instead, it aims only to get you thinking about one of the most important and fascinating topics you could ever hope to encounter: human language. Nothing is more important to us than language, and I hope this little book will quickly persuade you that nothing is more interesting, more stimulating or more rewarding than the study of language.

I have chosen eight very different aspects of the study of language, and under each heading I present and discuss a representative sample of the work which has been done and which is being done now. You will discover that you know a great deal more about the grammar of English than you ever suspected, but you may also be surprised to find that you can't explain the meaning of the word *dog*. You will learn about the astonishing way in which young children go about the business of learning their first language, about the startling effects on language of genetic defects and brain damage, and about people for whom words have colours. Perhaps you already know that the remote ancestor of English was spoken in Russia, but are you aware that English is changing fairly rapidly at this very moment, and that we can see it changing if we know how to watch?

By the time you've finished this book, you will know something about the mother-in-law languages of Australia, about the amazing gender systems of Navaho, Swahili and Dyirbal, about the strange arrangements the Norwegians have made for their language, and about why plumbers sound different from lawyers; you'll learn the truth about those Eskimo words for 'snow', and you'll find out why a universal translator is impossible. You'll learn how we can express meanings that aren't actually there, find out why some questions are impossible to ask in English, and find out how the harmless little word *nurse* can wreck a social occasion.

Some of the work I discuss was done decades ago, but most of it has been done only very recently, sometimes so recently that you will hardly be able to find an account of it elsewhere.

At the end of each chapter, I suggest some further reading for pursuing the topics that particularly engage your interest; the complete list of references is given in the bibliography at the end of the book.

I hope you enjoy reading this book as much as I've enjoyed writing it!

Acknowledgements

I am grateful to Claire L'Enfant and Julia Hall of Routledge for persuading me that I was the right person to write this book. Dick Hudson and two anonymous readers read early drafts of some of the chapters, and Lisa Wale read a draft of the whole book; I am grateful for their helpful comments, most of which I have managed to incorporate into the final version. My thanks, too, to all those colleagues who responded to my requests for information on the Linguist List. Naturally, all remaining shortcomings are the fault of my bridge partner.

Chapter 1

The uniqueness of human language

If you were asked to name the trait which most decisively distinguishes human beings from all other creatures on the planet, what would you choose? Love? Warfare? Art and music? Technology? Perhaps. But most people who have considered this question at length have come up with a single answer: *language*.

As I shall try to demonstrate, human language is arguably the single most remarkable characteristic that we have, the one that most truly sets our species apart. Our faculty of language, which we usually take for granted, exhibits a number of properties which are remarkable, even astonishing. Without language, we could hardly have created the human world we know. Our development of everything from music to warfare could never have come about in the absence of language. More than any other single characteristic, then, language is what makes us human. And human language is unique.

At first glance, this uniqueness may be far from obvious. After all, nearly every creature on the planet seems to have some kind of signalling system, some way of communicating with other members of the same species and occasionally even with members of other species. Crickets chirp, birds sing, monkeys squawk, fireflies flash, and even ants leave smelly trails for their co-workers to follow. And no doubt you are convinced that Rover or Tiddles has a special sort of 'woof' or 'meow' that means 'I'm hungry' or 'I want to go out'. Moreover, recent work by ethologists (people who study animal behaviour) has revealed that many animal signalling systems are far more interesting than was once thought. You may be aware, for example, that certain species of whales are now known to sing songs, or that honeybees perform elaborate dances to announce the location of nectar to the hive.

Fascinating as these discoveries are, however, and however much they may remind us not to take our fellow creatures for granted, the fact is that human language is so utterly different from all these other signalling systems that we are obliged to treat it as a thing apart: a truly unique phenomenon.

In this book, I shall try to explain some of the fascinating and astonishing things we have discovered about language. I begin with some of the fundamental properties which are often collectively known as the **design features** of language. One of these design features is absolutely crucial to the very existence of language.

Duality of patterning

For most people, most of the time, the ordinary medium of language is speech. How do we speak? Easy: we allow air from the lungs to pass out through our mouths, and at the same time we move our mouths in various ways to produce **speech sounds** – consonants and vowels. Every utterance we make consists of a sequence of speech sounds, one after the other.

But here's an interesting question: how many *different* speech sounds can you produce? Different enough, that is, that the person you're talking to will have no trouble in telling them apart.

Well, there is no cut-and-dried answer to this question: it depends on just how much difference you want to insist on. But the number is certainly not large. Unless you've had specialist training in

phonetics (the study of speech sounds), you will probably find it very difficult to produce even a hundred different individual sounds. (Remember, we're talking about *individual* sounds here, not sequences of sounds.) In fact, every human language operates with a much smaller set of speech sounds than this. Let's take a look at English.

Consider the word *cat*. How many speech sounds does it contain? Well, the English spelling system is not very trustworthy on questions like this, but here the spelling does suggest the right answer: three. They are the '*k*-sound', the 'flat *a*', and the '*t*-sound'. For convenience, let us introduce special symbols for these speech sounds: /k/, /æ/ and /t/, respectively. We use the slashes to indicate that we are talking about the distinctive speech sounds of a particular language – in this case, English. These distinctive speech sounds are called the **phonemes** of the language. Thus, in terms of the phonemes of English, the word *cat* can be represented as /kæt/.

Now, if someone asks you what the English word /kæt/ means, you will have no trouble in answering. But suppose someone asks you instead what the English phoneme /k/ means? This time it is impossible to answer, for the phoneme /k/ in fact has *no* meaning in English. Nor does any other phoneme: /æ/ and /t/ are just as meaningless as /k/.

But now notice something else: these same meaningless phonemes can be rearranged to produce different words with different meanings. Thus, the order /tæk/ produces the word *tack*, while /ækt/ gives *act*, /æt/ gives *at*, and /tækt/ gives *tact* or *tacked*. (Note that *tact* and *tacked*, in spite of their different spellings and different structures, are pronounced identically by most speakers of English.)

Let's add one more phoneme to our set: the '*p*-sound', or /p/. Now we can form the word /pæt/ *pat*, as well as /tæp/ *tap*, /pæk/ *pack*, /kæp/ *cap*, /pækt/ *pact* or *packed*, /tæpt/ *tapped*, /æpt/ *apt*, /kæpt/ *capped*, and quite a few others. You can see what's going on: by combining a very small set of meaningless speech sounds in various ways, we can produce a very large number of different meaningful items: words. All human languages are constructed in this way, and this type of structure is called **duality of patterning**, or **duality** for short. Duality is the use of a small number of meaningless elements in combination to produce a large number of meaningful elements.

Why is this type of structure so significant? Well, just imagine what the alternative would be. Suppose we had no meaningless sound units to work with – suppose instead that every individual sound we could produce had its own meaning. What would be the consequence of such an arrangement? It's obvious: *the number of different meanings we could express would be no greater than the number of different sounds we could produce*. And, since we have already seen that we can't produce more than about a hundred different speech sounds, the result would be that a language could only contain about a hundred 'words'. And this would be catastrophic: imagine an 'English' consisting of no more than a hundred words. It is not remotely possible that, with such a drastically limited vocabulary, we could do most of the things we do with English: we couldn't explain to the mechanic what's wrong with our car, we couldn't tell our children stories about rabbits or elves, we couldn't organize elections or negotiate treaties, we couldn't charm our way into another person's heart with seductive conversation, and we certainly couldn't write books about language.

'So what?' you may be asking at this stage. Why am I making such a song and dance about duality? Isn't it the obvious way to go about things? Maybe so, but here's the crux: *no other species on earth has a signalling system based on duality*. Duality is unique to human language. (In fact, bird songs and whale songs arguably contain an element of duality, but these are not exactly signalling systems.)

What do other creatures do, then? They do what we have just declared unthinkable for human language: their signalling systems are based on the principle of 'one sound, one meaning'. That is, a typical non-human animal will have one sound meaning, perhaps, 'This is my territory', and another meaning 'Look out – danger in the air', and perhaps a few more. But that's it – the total number of different things such a creature can 'say' is no larger than the number of different sounds available. In practice, the number of different signals, or *calls*, used by any given species is usually between three and six – though vervet monkeys have the remarkable total of twenty or so. And this, it should be obvious by now, is a stupendous difference. Some of the other important characteristics of language that we will be discussing are only made possible by this fundamental property of duality.

Incidentally, perhaps you are wondering just how many phonemes there are in English all together. The answer: forty-odd. Why such a vague answer? Because not all English speakers use exactly the same set of speech sounds. For example, do you pronounce the words *buck* and *book* differently or identically? People who pronounce them differently have one more vowel than those who pronounce them identically. How about *hair* and *air*? People who pronounce these differently have one more consonant than those who pronounce them identically. The same goes for *cot* and *caught*, *three* and *free*, *pull* and *pool*, *fur* and *fair*, and *poor* and *pour*. Similarly, people for whom *singer* and *finger* do not rhyme have one more consonant than those for whom they do rhyme. (You may be a little surprised to learn that some people make a distinction you don't make, or fail to make one you do make, but that's the way things are.) However, very few English-speakers have fewer than about forty phonemes, or more than about forty-five.

Other languages differ in the number of phonemes they use. At one extreme, the Brazilian language Piraha has only ten (seven consonants and three vowels), while, at the other, some languages of the Caucasus have at least eighty (most of them consonants). The average number seems to be around twenty-five, so that English, with its forty-odd, is a little above average. But, regardless of the number of speech sounds used, every human language is built on the principle of duality of patterning, a principle which is absolutely unique to us in the natural world, and a principle without which language as we know it could not exist.

Displacement and open-endedness

Displacement is the use of language to talk about things other than the here and now. We have not the slightest difficulty in talking about last night's football game, or our own childhood, or the behaviour of dinosaurs which lived over 100 million years ago, or the ultimate fate of the universe; with equal ease, we can discuss political events in Peru or the surface of the planet Neptune.

Open-endedness is our ability to use language to say anything at all, including lots of things we've never said or heard before. Here are a few English sentences:

(1.1) I find that polythene banjo strings give a most unsatisfactory twang.

(1.2) Luxembourg has invaded New Zealand.

(1.3) A large pink spider wearing sunglasses and wielding a feather duster boogied across the floor.

(1.4) Shakespeare wrote his plays in Swahili, and they were translated into English by his African bodyguards.

It is most unlikely that you have ever encountered any of these sentences before, and yet you have not the slightest difficulty in understanding them – even if you don't believe all of them. Nor do you have any more difficulty in producing totally new English sentences whenever you need them. In fact, most of the things you say and hear every day are completely new to you, and may never before have been uttered by anyone.

Both of these phenomena, our ability to talk about places and things far away in space and time, and our ability to produce and understand new utterances virtually without limit, are so familiar to us that we never give them a moment's thought. And yet they are truly remarkable. Remarkable – and absolutely vital. Can you imagine being able to talk about nothing but the present moment and about nothing but what you can see as you speak? Equally, can you imagine speaking a language that consisted only of a fixed list of possible utterances, so that, every time you opened your mouth, you could do no more than choose one utterance from that list? Such a 'language' would be inconceivably far away from what we understand languages to be.

And yet this unthinkable state of affairs is exactly the way animal signalling systems appear to be. With one striking and famous exception, discussed below, non-human animals do not exhibit displacement. So far as we can tell, mice do not swap stories about their close encounters with cats, nor do bears soberly discuss the severity of the coming winter. Rabbits do not engage in heated arguments about what might lie on the far side of the hill, nor do geese draw up plans for their next migration. Virtually all 'utterances' by non-human animals appear to relate directly, and exclusively, to the time and place of uttering.

Furthermore, these creatures exhibit nothing we could call open-endedness. Instead, it appears to be genuinely the case that each species' signalling system contains only a small number of possible utterances, and that nothing can be expressed beyond the limited range of possibilities available. A monkey may be able to say 'Look out – eagle' if that message is available in the system, but that same monkey cannot introduce any novelties: he cannot, for example, come up with an unprecedented 'Look out – two hunters with rifles', or, still less, on spotting his first Land Rover, 'Hey, everybody – what do you suppose that is?'

Of course, given the absence of duality, it could hardly be otherwise: we have already seen that duality is essential in a system that can express more than a small number of different meanings. Lacking duality, non-human creatures appear to be locked into a world of expression which we can barely conceive of: a system of communication lacking both a past and a future, bounded by the horizon, and devoid of novelties, consisting only of the endless repetition of a few familiar messages about what's going on at the moment.

There is, however, one striking exception to this bleak picture: we know of one creature whose signalling system conspicuously exhibits displacement, apparently uniquely in the non-human world. What is this remarkable creature? Not the chimpanzee, or the dolphin, as you might have guessed: it's the common honeybee.

In the 1950s and 1960s, the Austrian ethologist Karl von Frisch carried out a series of studies which revealed something unexpected about the behaviour of European honeybees. When a honeybee scout discovers a useful source of nectar, it flies back to its hive and then performs an astonishing little dance inside, watched by the other bees. The details of the dance vary depending both on the distance to the nectar and on the particular species and variety of bee (honeybees have 'dialects'!). In the most famous case, though, the dancing bee performs a 'tail-wagging dance' in the form of a squashed figure eight with a straight middle section. Von Frisch was able to decode this dance, as follows. The time the dancing bee takes to complete a circuit of the figure eight indicates the distance to the nectar source: a longer time represents a longer flight. The level of excitement

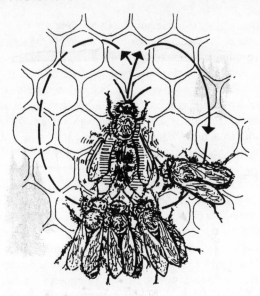

FIGURE 1.1 The tail-wagging dance
Source: Reprinted with permission from A. Akmajian, R.A. Demers and R.M. Harmish (1979) *Linguistics: An Introduction to Language and Communication*, Cambridge, MA: MIT Press, p. 12.

demonstrated by the bee represents the quantity of nectar, and hence the number of bees needed to harvest it: greater excitement, more nectar, and hence more bees needed. Finally, and most stunningly, the orientation of the straight part of the figure eight represents the direction of the source with respect to the position of the sun: for example, if the straight section is oriented at 80° to the left of straight up, the bees will fly toward a point 80° to the left of the sun. (See Figures 1.1 and 1.2.)

Now this is displacement. The dancing bee is passing on information about a nectar source which it visited some time ago, which is now perhaps miles away, and which it therefore cannot see. Moreover, the watching bees clearly understand that they are being informed about a task which they should perform in the (near) future. And the system is extremely effective: von Frisch found that his bees could regularly locate nectar sources up to about seven miles away

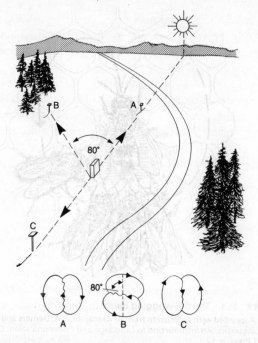

FIGURE 1.2 The dances which send worker bees to three feeding stations A, B and C
Source: Reprinted with permission from A. Akmajian, R.A. Demers and R.M. Harmish (1979) *Linguistics: An Introduction to Language and Communication*, Cambridge, MA: MIT Press, p. 13.

(about eleven kilometres). This is impressive. How successful do you think you'd be at finding a particular cluster of bushes seven miles away after being given only oral directions?

Wonderful as the bee dance is, it is none the less, as von Frisch was able to show, severely limited in important respects. In a famous experiment, he allowed some scouts to find an artificial nectar source, a bowl of sugar and water, placed on top of a pole twenty feet high, much higher than the bees were accustomed to finding nectar. The scouts returned to the hive and danced as usual. The result? A swarm of bees soon arrived at the pole, buzzed around it in seeming confusion for a while, and then went home. The dancing scouts had been utterly unable to include in their dance the novel bit of information about the height – or, as von Frisch put it, there is no word in honeybee for 'up'.

The honeybee dance is astounding, and we are forced to admit that at least one creature besides human beings can exhibit displacement in communication. But we must not let our amazement obscure some hard facts. The honeybee dance is unique in the animal world; no other creature has anything similar, not even other insects. And that dance is severely restricted in its communicative power: it cannot cope with the slightest novelty. Apart from its undoubted displacement, the bee dance is just as limited in its expressive power as any other animal signalling system. Bees have nothing that we would recognize as language.

Stimulus-freedom

Related to some of the preceding design features, but none the less partially distinct, is the property of **stimulus-freedom**, which is the ability to say anything you like in any context. Suppose someone says to you 'What do you think of my skirt?' You are free to make any response you like, including none at all. You might reply 'It's too short', or 'It doesn't go with your pink blouse', or 'Sorry – I have no taste in clothes'. You can even decline to answer, and change the subject.

Of course, this doesn't mean that human conversation is utterly random. There are all sorts of social pressures that make some responses more likely than others. If you value the friendship of the woman in the skirt, you are most unlikely to reply 'God, Julia, my dog's blanket would look better – you have the worst taste in clothes in the Northern Hemisphere'. Even if you're thinking that, you probably wouldn't say it. But you *could* say it if you wanted to: there's nothing about English that prevents you, but merely social conventions and the desire to maintain good relationships.

The absence of stimulus-freedom would once again reduce human language to something unrecognizable. Just try to imagine a world in which your every remark was completely determined by the context, so that, like a character in a play, you never had the slightest choice of what to say. There are, of course, certain formal and especially ceremonial contexts in which something like this actually does happen – church services, Passover meals, the taking of oaths – but such contexts are not the norm, and even there you could, in principle, say something unexpected, if at the cost of ruining your position in society.

By now you are probably expecting to hear that stimulus-freedom too is unique to human language, and I shall not disappoint you. Non-human signals are not stimulus-free, but rather **stimulus-bound**. That is, a non-human creature produces a particular signal always and only when the appropriate stimulus is present. If Fred the monkey is up a tree, and he sees a dangerous eagle approaching, he automatically produces the cry that means 'Look out – eagle!', and he never does this at any other time. He doesn't, on spotting the eagle, think to himself 'Maybe if I keep quiet the eagle will grab old Charlie down there, and I'll be safe'. Nor does a bored Fred suddenly come out with an eagle warning and then guffaw 'Haw, haw, Charlie – gotcha that time!'

Very occasionally, however, an animal has been observed to do something unusual. For example, an Arctic fox was once spotted making a danger call in the absence of any danger, apparently just to distract her cubs from a meal she was trying to eat. But such incidents are, so far at least, very rare and strictly anecdotal: they do not represent normal behaviour, which is overwhelmingly stimulus-bound.

Lacking duality, lacking displacement, lacking open-endedness, lacking stimulus-freedom, animal signalling systems are almost unfathomably different from human languages. The communicative world in which other creatures live is as different from ours as anything we could imagine: from our point of view, bleak, featureless, closed in on every side. As I said at the beginning of this chapter, human language is unique on earth, and without it we could not count ourselves human at all.

Arbitrariness

In addition to the design features which set human language well apart from animal signalling systems, there are others which are not unique at all, but none the less worthy of attention. Chief among these is **arbitrariness**, which is the absence of any *necessary* connection between a linguistic form and its meaning.

Note that word *necessary*. I am certainly not suggesting that there is no connection at all between the English word *pig* and the large snouted animal to which we commonly apply it. Of course there's a connection, but it's an *arbitrary* connection. There is no *a priori* reason why English speakers should apply the particular sound sequence *pig* to that particular animal: the connection is purely a matter of agreement, and the word can be successfully used only so long as English speakers agree to use it in this particular way. Speakers of other languages, of course, have reached different agreements, but no word is intrinsically better suited to naming this particular animal than any other, though each is perfectly adequate as long as speakers agree about it.

Such agreement need not be for all time. The animal was formerly called a *swine* in English, but this older word is now little used except as a light-hearted insult, and *pig* has replaced it as the name of the animal. The decision as to which words shall have which meanings is entirely a matter of convention. Different languages have different conventions (that's part of the reason they *are* different languages), and conventions can and do change.

Arbitrariness can be demonstrated the other way round. The English word *mean* has several different meanings – or, more accurately, there are several different English words sharing the form *mean*. The French word *mine* sounds almost exactly like English *mean*, but the French word means '(coal)mine'. Likewise, Welsh *min* means 'edge', Basque *min* means 'pain', and Arabic *min* means 'from'. There is nothing about this sequence of sounds that makes any one meaning more natural than another.

The overwhelming presence of arbitrariness in language is the chief reason it takes so long to learn the vocabulary of a foreign language: it's generally impossible to guess the meaning of an unfamiliar word, and each new word just has to be learned individually. Even if I give you the big clue that all of the following Basque words are the names of living creatures, I very much doubt that you'll be able to guess any of them: *zaldi, igel, txori, oilo, behi, sagu*. In fact, they mean 'horse', 'frog', 'bird', 'hen', 'cow' and 'mouse', respectively.

This arbitrariness is the reason that the 'universal translator' beloved of science-fiction B movies is simply impossible. You know the scene: our intrepid space adventurers arrive on a new planet and find an alien race speaking a totally unfamiliar language, so they whip out their machine and twiddle a couple of dials, and – hey presto! – the alien speech is at once rendered into perfect American English. Because of arbitrariness, even the most powerful computer can have no way of knowing whether the alien utterance *Kwarfnigli* means 'Welcome to our planet', or 'Prepare to be sacrificed to the Great God Kwarf', or 'You've parked your space ship in a tow-away zone', or perhaps even 'Hey, Edna – come and look at these weirdos'. On a more realistic scale, even if you learn a couple of thousand Basque words, if someone says to you 'Watch out – you might run into a *lupu* out there', where *lupu* is a word you don't know, you have no way of knowing whether a *lupu* might be a bear trap, a poisonous snake, an armed robber or a starving wolf. In fact, it's a scorpion – though in a now extinct dialect of Basque, recorded in the sixteenth century, an identical word *lupu* meant 'wolf'. So much for the universal translator.

Arbitrariness is in no way unique to human language: it is typical of animal signalling systems and of virtually every conceivable system of communication. But, occasionally, in language and elsewhere, we find elements which are not entirely arbitrary, but rather somewhat iconic. **Iconicity** is a direct correlation between form and meaning. We saw some iconic elements in the bee dance, in which a time represents a time and an angle represents an angle. But English, too, has some iconic elements.

The most familiar examples of iconicity in English are provided by instances of **onomatopoeia** – the representation of sounds by words of similar sound. Such words as *splash, clink, buzz, meow, moan, whoosh, thud, moo, ping, quack* and *boom* all represent attempts to reproduce real-world sounds with English phonemes. But even these onomatopoeic items still exhibit a great deal of arbitrariness in their forms. The easiest way to see this is to compare onomatopoeic items from several languages. The sound of a gunshot is represented in English as *bang*, in Spanish as *pum*, in French as *pan*, in German as *peng*, and in Basque as *dzast*.

In fact, onomatopoeic words are so strongly arbitrary that they have to be learned individually, just like ordinary words. Can you guess the meaning of Japanese *chirin-chirin*? It means 'tinkle'. How about Turkish *şip*? It means 'plop'. Turkish *şak*? It's 'clap' or 'crack'. Hebrew *yimyum*? It's 'meow' (!) Basque *kukurruku*? Easy, this one: it's 'cock-a-doodle-do'. Japanese *pyuu*? It's 'whizz'.

There is another, much more subtle, type of iconicity in language. Suppose I tell you that the Basque word *tximeleta* (pronounced, roughly, chee-may-LAY-tah) is also the name of a creature. What sort of creature do you suppose a *tximeleta* might be? Large or small? Fast or slow? Pretty or ugly? Any thoughts? Now suppose I tell you further that *tximeleta* means one of the following: 'fox', 'bull', 'butterfly', 'snail', 'tortoise'. Which do you suppose it is?

Well, I was hoping you'd guessed it by now. Most people find that the word *tximeleta* seems to suggest, not something large or ponderous or slow, but rather something small and light and fluttery, and so they correctly pick out the only small, light, fluttery creature in the list.

This is not onomatopoeia, because the form of the word *tximeleta* is not in any way related to the sound of anything – butterflies don't even make any sound. Rather, the sound of the word seems somehow to correlate with the *appearance* of the insect: the word sounds light and fluttery, and the butterfly looks light and fluttery. This type of iconicity is sometimes called **phonaesthesia**, and both phonaesthesia and onomatopoeia are varieties of what is more generally called **sound symbolism**. All types of sound symbolism are partial exceptions to the more usual arbitrariness of language, but sound symbolism is a special case, and arbitrariness is the norm.

The vocal tract

As I mentioned above, the primary medium of language is speech – that is, the production of sequences of speech sounds. Speech is performed by allowing air from the lungs to pass up and out through the mouth and nose. Of course, speech is not the only possible medium for language. If you're reading this book, you'll be aware that language can be transferred, with a high degree of success, into the medium of **writing** – though this transfer is a recent development in the history of human language. The oldest known written texts are less than 6,000 years old, while speech, as we shall see later, is very considerably older than that, and even now the great majority of the world's 5,000 or so languages are not normally written down. Far more recent still is the invention of **sign language**, in which language is transferred to the medium of gestures made chiefly with the hands; this too we shall be discussing below.

But speech is the primary medium, and human beings have evolved in such a way as to make efficient speech possible. The passageway through which air flows as we speak is called the **vocal tract**, and the human vocal tract is highly unusual, even unique, among mammals. Even our closest relatives, the apes, have vocal tracts which are quite different from ours and which are not very different from the vocal tracts of, say, horses or mice. Take a look at Figures 1.3 and 1.4, showing cross-sections of the vocal tracts of a person and of a chimpanzee.

There are several significant differences. For one thing, the human vocal tract is much larger and differently shaped: it extends well down behind the back of the tongue. Further, there is a big difference in the connection between the **trachea**, or windpipe, which leads to the lungs, and the **oesophagus**, or gullet, which leads to the stomach. In the chimp, as in most mammals, a large cartilage called the **epiglottis** serves as a kind of valve between the two. When the epiglottis is raised (as shown), the trachea is connected to the nose and the mouth is sealed off. When the epiglottis is lowered, the mouth is connected to the oesophagus, and the trachea is sealed off. This useful arrangement makes it virtually impossible for a chimp to choke on its food.

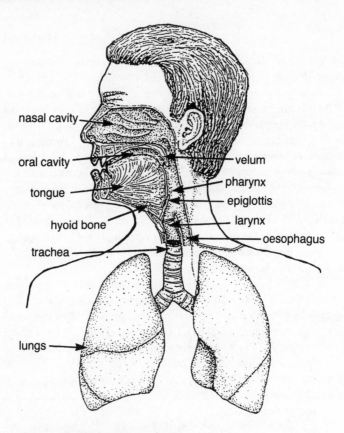

FIGURE 1.3 The human vocal tract
Source: Reprinted and adapted with permission from P. Lieberman (1991) *Uniquely Human: The Evolution of Speech, Thought and Selfless Behavior*, Cambridge, MA: Harvard University Press, p. 40.

The human being, however, is not so fortunate. The long part of the vocal tract called the **pharynx** is common to both the flow of air and the passage of food, and the small human epiglottis is not very effective at sealing off the trachea during swallowing. As a result, it is very easy for us to choke on our food, and dozens of people die this way every year in Britain alone. Why have human beings, almost

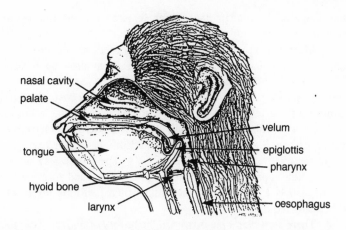

FIGURE 1.4 The vocal tract of the chimpanzee
Source: Reprinted and adapted with permission from P. Lieberman (1991) *Uniquely Human: The Evolution of Speech, Thought and Selfless Behavior*, Cambridge, MA: Harvard University Press, p. 55.

uniquely among mammals, evolved this dangerous arrangement? Why have we not retained the safer vocal tract of our ancestors?

Even more intriguing is the fact that newborn human babies have vocal tracts which resemble that of the chimpanzee, and young babies are therefore protected against choking to death. Only after about three months does the infant's growth stretch its vocal tract into the dangerous adult shape. It looks as if evolution has really worked very hard at rearranging our vocal tract into its present curious shape. But why?

Dangerous or not, the human vocal tract has one great advantage: since it is so large and elongated, it allows us to produce a number of speech sounds – at least some dozens of distinct consonants and vowels, as you'll recall. But the chimpanzee vocal tract and the vocal tract of a newborn baby lack this ability. Investigation has shown that the chimp vocal tract can scarcely produce more than one vowel and a couple of consonants. And this is not nearly enough to allow speech and language. Recall that we need to have a range of speech sounds at our disposal in order to take

17

advantage of the fundamental design feature of duality: no speech sounds, no duality, and no duality, no language.

Many investigators have therefore reached the conclusion that our vocal tracts have evolved very specifically to allow us to speak. The idea is that speech and language proved to be so beneficial to the species that we became specialized for it even at the cost of losing a number of our fellows to death by choking every year. Intimately related to the evolution of our distinctive vocal tract would have been the accompanying evolution of our remarkably big brain. The use of language requires not only the ability to speak but also a very considerable capacity for rapid mental processing – and apes, we now know, also lack that part of the brain which performs the mental processing required for speaking.

There are several landmarks in the history of human evolution. Our upright posture (for which we have paid the price of frequent problems with our backs) and our hands, with our skilful fingers and especially our opposable thumbs, were of course vital developments – but these, as we now know, were evolved millions of years ago by ancestors who had not yet acquired large brains and probably not our distinctive vocal tract. More than any other development in our history, the development of speech and language set us apart from our ancestors and from our relatives, and put us, for better or for worse, on the path to our uniquely human behaviour. Indeed, several specialists have suggested that, rather than calling our species in Latin *Homo sapiens* 'the wise human', we might better call ourselves *Homo loquens* 'the speaking human'.

And just when did human language evolve? No one knows. Almost everyone agrees that language has been around for at least 100,000 years or so, which is when we find the first evidence of fully modern humans indistinguishable from ourselves. A minority of scholars would suggest a much earlier origin, going back perhaps to our immediate ancestor, *Homo erectus*, over a million years ago. The topic is controversial, of course, since we have practically nothing in the way of evidence.

One famous attempt at tackling the question has been made by the speech scientists Philip Lieberman and Edmund Crelin in a series of publications. Their work concerns the Neandertals (or Neanderthals), a somewhat distinctive stockily built people who inhabited western Europe until around 35,000 years ago, when they abruptly vanished, possibly under pressure from our own direct ancestors. Working with a fossilized Neandertal skull, Lieberman and Crelin have proposed a reconstruction of the Neandertal vocal tract, and their reconstruction shows a vocal tract very different from ours and more akin to that of a chimpanzee. Lieberman and Crelin therefore conclude that the Neandertals could not have produced an adequate range of speech sounds and hence could not have spoken.

Fascinating though this attempt is, Lieberman and Crelin's conclusions have been fiercely attacked on various grounds. For one thing, the (crushed) skull they used had been improperly reassembled by an earlier worker. For another, it appears that several different reconstructions are possible even after the skull is restored to its proper shape, including some which look much more like modern human vocal tracts, and some critics have argued that Lieberman and Crelin's reconstruction would not even have allowed the owner of the skull to open his mouth. The question, therefore, remains open. We do not know when language appeared, though most specialists would guess a date much less than a million years ago.

Signing chimps

In the last several decades, a number of researchers have attempted to look at the question of language origins from a very different direction. Even though, as I have stressed in this chapter, language is clearly unique to humans, we might still ask the following question: could a non-human animal learn a human language if it had the chance?

This question has inspired a great number of experiments, some of which have occasionally attracted headlines in the news. What many (not all) of the investigators have attempted is to bring a baby animal into a human household, to bring it up as far as possible like a human baby, to surround it with language, and to encourage it to use language itself. But this obvious approach presents some formidable difficulties. For one thing, not all baby animals can be fitted into a human household. Dolphins and killer whales are known to be highly intelligent, but it is scarcely possible to bring up a baby killer whale in your living room. For this reason, most experimenters have worked with baby apes, usually chimpanzees, occasionally gorillas. With their humanoid form, baby apes can be accommodated in human surroundings. Just as importantly, apes (especially chimps) are our closest living relatives, and hence we might expect that, if any other creatures could learn human language, it would be apes.

But apes, as we have seen, lack a human vocal tract, and hence there is no possibility of teaching them to speak. This blunt fact defeated the first experiments with the chimps Gua and Viki. However, we have already noted that speech is not the only possible medium for language, and it's not even the only one that human beings use. Deaf people have difficulty in producing and under-standing speech, and in the nineteenth century several systems were invented to assist them. These were systems of **sign language**, in which the user, or *signer*, communicates with gestures made mostly with the hands. For example, in American Sign Language, or ASL, the version used in the USA, putting the tip of the thumb to the lips means 'drink', while pulling the thumb and two fingers away from the upper lip means 'cat'. Like other versions of sign language (including British Sign Language (BSL), a similar system employing a different set of signs), ASL is widely used by deaf people, who often become extremely fluent in using it. There are even children of deaf parents whose first language is sign language and who are therefore 'native signers'. Now sign language is not just a crude approximation to language, as was formerly thought, nor is it merely a coded version of English. In recent years linguists have discovered that the sign language used by native signers appears to possess *all* of the crucial characteristics of human language, including rich grammatical sys-tems with things like subordinate clauses and verbal inflections – and apes have hands closely resembling our own.

In the 1960s the psychologists Allen and Beatrice Gardner introduced a young chimpanzee called Washoe into a group of adult human signers; these signers made every effort to encourage Washoe to understand and use signs. The results seemed so encouraging that further chimps were added to the experiment, and other groups began similar experiments with chimpanzees or occasionally gorillas. Still other groups tried something similar, not with sign language, but with invented languages whose 'words' were coloured plastic magnets of varying shapes stuck on a board or geometric shapes displayed on a computer screen.

By the late 1960s and early 1970s most of these research groups were reporting impressive achievements by their animals. The animals were said to be capable of understanding hundreds of signs or symbols, of understanding and responding appropriately to new sentences made up of novel combinations of signs or symbols, of producing spontaneous utterances of their own, of understanding high-level abstractions, of coining new 'words' by original combinations of existing signs or symbols, and even of teaching sign language to their own offspring. These reports attracted much publicity and also a great deal of criticism.

The sceptics found no shortage of weaknesses in the evidence supporting the claims of the chimpanzee experimenters. First, much of that evidence proved to be purely anecdotal: that is, it consisted of reports that some particular animal on some particular occasion had been observed to do something-or-other pretty damned impressive. But anecdotal evidence is almost devoid of value in science: any single event can have any of a large number of explanations, most of them not very interesting, and only well-documented reports of *consistent* behaviour by an animal can be counted as substantial evidence. Second, many of the experimenters were found to have applied very generous standards in testing their animals. For example, if a signing chimp was shown an apple and asked (in ASL) 'What is this?', the experimenters frequently counted as a correct response any sequence of signs including the sign for 'apple', including something like 'yellow banana hungry me apple banana apple', which is a far cry from the sort of response usually heard from a human child learning a first language. Third, we have in many cases nothing more than the experimenters' own word for it that the apes were making any signs at all. In one case in which a native human signer was called in to check the animals' behaviour, he protested that he couldn't see *any* recognizable signs, but only meaningless gestures which were none the less being enthusiastically recorded as signs by the other humans present. Finally, and most damningly, the critics discovered that the experimental procedures typically used to test the animals were so slipshod that an animal under test could often see its human handler unconsciously forming the required response with her or his own hands, so that it could see what to do – a well-known phenomenon in working with animals, and known as the 'Clever Hans effect', after a nineteenth-century performing horse which could apparently answer questions in arithmetic but which was actually just watching its owner for clues as to what to do. When the experimental technique was tightened up, the performance of the animals became very much worse, and was often no better than chance.

As a result of these criticisms, some experimenters became disillusioned with the whole project of teaching language to animals, while others decided simply to shift their attention to studying the ordinary cognitive abilities of their animals, without trying to teach them novel types of behaviour. A few, however, gritted their teeth, tightened up their procedures, and returned to their efforts. Work in this field still continues today, and experimenters still report that their animals can learn to understand two or three hundred signs, though the performance of the animals seems to tail off rapidly after about this much, just at the point at which a human child's progress begins to accelerate almost explosively. Because of this, many people have concluded that the most important result we have obtained from all these projects is a vivid demonstration of the vast gulf that separates the linguistic behaviour of human children from that of all other creatures. Language, it seems, is still unique to human beings.

Further reading

The idea of design features was introduced by the American linguist Charles Hockett (Hockett 1960); both Hockett and others have occasionally proposed modifications to Hockett's original list of sixteen features, and several versions of the list can be found, but all include the important features discussed in this chapter. Lieberman and Crelin's work can be found in a number of places, of which Lieberman (1975 and 1984) are particularly convenient. The most recent work on the evolution of language is summarized in Hawkins and Gell-Mann (1992), while Leakey (1994) presents a popular account of human origins, including language origins, from the point of view of palaeoanthropology. For the signing chimps, see Linden (1974) or Savage-Rumbaugh (1986) for a favourable account and Sebeok and Umiker-Sebeok (1980) or Wallman (1992) for a critical review.

Chapter 2

The grammatical
backbone

One of the most important characteristics of language
is the presence of grammar. The **grammar** of a
language is simply the way it combines smaller
elements (such as words) into larger elements (such as
sentences). Every human language has a grammar;
indeed, every human language has quite a lot of
grammar. And I mean *every* language, without exception.

It is a grotesque error to believe that, somewhere
out there, there are languages with little or no grammar. Even the most remote languages, spoken by the
least technologically advanced peoples, have masses
and masses of grammar. Just to cite one example, John
Haiman's book describing the grammar of Hua, a
language spoken in a remote valley of New Guinea by
a people with stone-age technology who only made
contact with the outside world a few decades ago, runs
to many hundreds of dense pages, and Haiman would
certainly not claim that his description is complete.
The biggest descriptions of English grammar run to a

couple of thousand pages, and are unquestionably not complete even yet. (It's not that English has more grammar than Hua; it's just that English grammar has been studied for much longer and by far more people than the grammar of Hua.) Even artificial languages like Esperanto have masses of grammar, though in my experience the proponents of these languages often seem to be unaware of this fact.

Linguists (practitioners of **linguistics**, the scientific study of language) regard it as one of their central tasks to find out what the grammars of human languages are like. Linguists who specialize in the study of grammar are **grammarians**; what grammarians try to do is to identify the **rules of grammar** that govern each particular language.

We need to clarify this notion *rule of grammar*, since it is frequently misunderstood. Perhaps your school English teacher issued you with stern warnings like 'Don't end a sentence with a preposition', or 'Don't use a split infinitive', or 'You should say *It's I* and not *It's me*'. (Then again, maybe she didn't – not many schools try to teach much English grammar these days.) But statements like these, familiar or not, are *not* what I mean by 'rules of grammar'. They aren't really rules at all: they're merely someone's opinions about what constitutes good usage in English.

Rules are rather different. Consider the business of driving a car. When you press down on the accelerator, the car speeds up. When you step on the brake, the car slows down. When you turn the steering wheel to the left, the car goes left. These are some of the 'rules of driving' – that's just the way cars work, and you can't do much about it.

Opinions about good driving are things like 'Stop for a red light', 'Put the car in second gear when turning a corner' and 'Speed up when the light in front of you turns amber'. Of course, there's no guarantee that all of these opinions are *good* advice – and the same is true of English. There's no guarantee that the opinions about using English cited above are necessarily *good* opinions – and in fact I'll be arguing in Chapter 8 that all three of them are terrible opinions. Anyway, the rules of English grammar are something quite different from opinions about usage. Let's have a look at the grammar of English.

A first look at English grammar

You may sometimes have heard it said that 'English doesn't have much grammar'. This statement is grossly false: English, like every other language, has lots and lots of grammar. What English *doesn't* have, of course, is lots of word-endings. Unlike some other languages, English doesn't make much use of word-endings for grammatical purposes. But word-endings are only one part of grammar, and not a particularly large part at that.

Perhaps you get a sinking feeling in your stomach when I mention that English has masses of grammar. Perhaps the very word *grammar* turns you off. Perhaps you're convinced that you don't know anything about grammar, and you're afraid you'll never be able to understand all that technical stuff. If so, you are in for a big surprise: the fact is, you already know a huge amount of grammar. In fact, you know more about the grammar of your mother tongue than can be found in the pages of even the thickest book. Please bear with me, and I'll try to demonstrate the truth of this statement.

We begin with a simple illustration of some of the rules of English grammar. Consider example (2.1):

(2.1) There's a spider in the bath.

There's nothing remarkable about this example: it's a perfectly ordinary sentence of English, consisting of some perfectly ordinary English words. But, although there aren't many endings on view here, there is quite a bit of grammar. To see this, try putting the same words in a different order:

(2.2) *Bath the in spider a there's.

We use an asterisk to indicate that something is not a grammatical sentence. And this is certainly not a grammatical sentence of English: it's utter gibberish. Why? Because the words are in the wrong order. Word order is a very important part of English grammar: most of the time a speaker of English has very little freedom in choosing the order of words. The grammar of English requires them to go in a particular order, and that's that. But now look at the Basque translation of (2.1):

(2.3) Bainuan armiarma bat dago.
        bath-the-in spider a there's   (literally)

This Basque sentence is fully grammatical, according to the rules of Basque grammar. But it looks exactly like the English gibberish in (2.2), apart from the trivial difference that some of the things that are separate words in English are suffixes in Basque. What happens if we try to use the English order in Basque?

(2.4) *Dago bat armiarma -n -a bainu.

This is unspeakable gibberish in Basque. The grammars of both English and Basque contain rules specifying the order of elements, but those rules happen to be very different in the two languages. Apart from having different words for things, languages can also differ from one another in having different rules of grammar. Let's compare English and Basque a little further.

(2.5) John hit Peter.

This is another very ordinary English sentence. And here's its Basque translation:

(2.6) Jonek Kepa jo du.

(*Jon* and *Kepa* are the Basque forms of 'John' and 'Peter', and *jo du* is the verb 'hit'.) You will see that the Basque form is literally 'John Peter hit', which is impossible in English. Now let's switch the names:

(2.7) Peter hit John.

This is another grammatical English sentence, but of course it has a completely different meaning from (2.5). What happens if we switch the names in the Basque example?

(2.8) Kepa Jonek jo du.

This is also grammatical in Basque, but it does *not* mean 'Peter hit John'. Instead, it still means 'John hit Peter', just like (2.6) (though a better translation might be 'It was John who hit Peter'). In Basque, it makes much less difference than in English what order you put things in, because Basque, unlike English, makes extensive use of word-endings for grammatical purposes. In our examples, the ending *-ek* on the name *Jon* makes it clear that Jon is doing the hitting, and not Kepa, and so a Basque speaker can switch the words around a bit without changing the meaning significantly. English, with its lack of endings, uses word order to keep track of grammatical relations, and hence English word order is much more rigid than that of Basque.

Now let's leave Basque and look a little deeper into the grammar of English.

A rule of English grammar

Consider the next four sentences, all of them consisting of the same words and all of them having apparently very similar structures:

(2.9)   After Lisa got up, she had a shower.

(2.10) Lisa had a shower after she got up.

(2.11) After she got up, Lisa had a shower.

(2.12) She had a shower after Lisa got up.

Now, in a suitable context, the word *she* in every one of these sentences might possibly refer to some person not named in the sentence. But here's my question: in which of these four sentences could *she* possibly refer to Lisa?

It shouldn't take you long to decide on your answer, and almost certainly your answer is this: the word *she* can possibly refer to Lisa in the first three examples, but *not* in the last one. Agreed?

What's going on here? Why should the result be different only for the last example? Well, it's a matter of grammar. There is a rule of English grammar governing the use of words like *she* (which are called **pronouns**), and that rule is violated if you try to make *she* refer to Lisa in (2.12), but not in the other three examples.

This time we are looking at a genuine rule of grammar. This is not an expression of somebody's opinion about English usage. This is a basic fact about the way English works, about the way English is put together. You have never been explicitly taught this rule, and almost certainly you have never noticed it or thought about it before. In fact, *nobody* succeeded in stating this rule until the American linguist Ronald Langacker worked it out in 1969 – though it had, of course, been in the language for centuries. Yet, when you speak or hear English, you automatically apply it, and so you would never, for example, try to say (2.12) with *she* referring to Lisa. In some important sense, you know this rule, even if you can't state it. Just as the rules of driving a car are built into the car, this rule of grammar is built into the structure of English.

And what is this rule? No doubt you are waiting impatiently to see it. Well, I'll present it in just a moment, but first here's a warning: when you see it, you'll probably be very disappointed. Ready? Here it is:

(2.13) An anaphor may not both precede and command its antecedent.

You know the word *precede*, but *anaphor*, *command* and *antecedent* are very probably so much gobbledygook as far as you're concerned. Why do I insist on presenting this rule in such incomprehensible jargon? Why don't I just say it in plain English? Well, because it's very *hard* to say it in plain English. Still, I'll have a go. Here's an attempt at a 'plain English' version of the rule:

(2.14) A word (like *she*) that takes its meaning entirely from a
second word in the same sentence (like *Lisa*) cannot come
before that second word if that second word is inside a
subordinate clause.

Any better? In fact, this new version is far less satisfactory than the original version: it's longer, it's clumsier, it's less general, and, worst of all, it's less accurate, since it misses out a few crucial details. But you can perhaps now get some idea what (2.13) says, though only if you know what a subordinate clause is. Like *anaphor* and *command*, *subordinate clause* is a technical term in the study of grammar, though a much older one, and perhaps you're familiar with it. If you're not, no doubt you'd like me to explain it. But that's not so simple. To explain what a subordinate clause is, I would first have to explain what a *clause* is; to explain what a clause is, I would first have to explain what a *finite verb* is; to explain what a finite verb is, I would first have to explain what a *verb* is; and so on.

You see the problem. The grammar of a language is a complex and highly structured affair, and it operates in terms of concepts and categories which have to be defined in terms of other concepts and categories, which themselves have to be defined in the same way. Consequently, the only way to make progress in investigating grammar is to start with a suitable set of basic terms and then to use them to define further terms, which are then available for defining still more complex terms, and so on. If I tried to replace the term *subordinate clause* in (2.14) with a complete definition all the way down to the simplest concepts imaginable, the result would take up a whole page or more, and it would be unreadable. Technical terms are unavoidable – though they must, of course, be *suitable* technical terms.

In this respect, the study of grammar, or indeed the study of language in general, is no different from the serious study of anything else. Anyone who studies physics, or music, or psychology, or genetics, or any class of complex phenomena, is obliged to build up layers of increasingly complex concepts and to give those concepts names, in the form of technical terms – otherwise, the whole subject just becomes unmanageable.

Curiously, many people who unhesitatingly accept this fact as valid for physics or music are inclined to reject it for the study of language, and to complain bitterly that linguists (and especially grammarians) deliberately try to make their subject opaque to outsiders with masses of pointless jargon and mysterious algebraic symbols; they often take the view that grammar is just a matter of 'common sense', and that we can and should say everything in 'plain English'. Well, they're wrong. Language is not simple, and grammar is not simple, and a grammarian can no more do without technical terms than a nuclear physicist can.

But the technical terms are only essential for *stating* the rules of grammar. You probably don't know all these technical terms, but don't let that trivial point conceal the fact that you certainly *do* know the rules of English grammar. For example, you know Langacker's rule, and you always obey it when you speak and when you listen to other people. Isn't that interesting? And there you were thinking that you didn't know any English grammar.

Knowing how to speak a language is rather like knowing how to ride a bicycle, or how to ice skate, or how to tie a shoelace, except that speaking a language is much more complicated than any of these other activities. You know how to apply all the rules, even if you can't state them. You can ride a bike perfectly well without being able to explain why the bike stays up: that's a job for a physicist, who may need to invoke a rather daunting collection of terms and equations to describe what you're doing. In much the same way, a linguist needs to invoke a rather daunting collection of technical terms in order to describe accurately just what you're doing when you speak English.

Before we leave Langacker's rule, let me reiterate one point. Unlike the English teacher who tells you not to split infinitives, Langacker was not expressing an *opinion* about anything. He was not suggesting that it would be a good idea to follow his rule, or that people would look down their noses at you if you didn't follow it. Langacker was simply stating a rule that already existed in the English of all native speakers. In other words, Langacker *discovered* a fact about English, a rule of English grammar that was already there waiting to be discovered. Langacker was probably not the first person who ever noticed that the last example was different from the first three, but he was the first person to figure out exactly what was going on. And figuring out what is going on in language is precisely the business that linguists are in.

Another rule

Lest you think that Langacker's rule might be a special case, let's look at another rule of English grammar. I'll call this one 'Ross's rule', because it was first identified by the American linguist John Ross in 1967. Consider the following simple sentence:

(2.15) Lisa bought a car.

Nothing remarkable here, or so it seems. Now, I'm going to construct a question that asks about that car by using the phrase *which car*:

(2.16) Which car did Lisa buy?

This sentence illustrates the usual way of forming questions in

English, which in fact is rather complicated: the phrase *which car* has to come at the beginning of the sentence, whereas *a car* in (2.15) came at the end; the word *did* pops up; we have *buy* instead of *bought*; and so on. If you don't think this is complicated, ask someone who's learned English as a foreign language. But Ross's rule does not concern the way in which questions are formed, but rather the circumstances in which it's possible to form a question at all. Let's try to do the same thing with some further examples:

(2.17) Tim said Lisa told him Larry bought a car yesterday.

(2.18) Which car did Tim say Lisa told him Larry bought yesterday?

(2.19) She was describing a car to the police when it suddenly drove past.

(2.20) Which car was she describing to the police when it suddenly drove past?

(2.21) The guests who arrived in a car are ready to go home.

(2.22) *Which car are the guests who arrived in ready to go home?

Oops! Something has gone wrong with this last one. But why? I've followed all the usual rules for making English questions – and yet the result is no good. It's not a grammatical sentence of English. In fact, there is absolutely *no* way of asking the question that the ungrammatical (2.22) is trying to ask – that is, there is no question that correlates with the statement in (2.21), in complete contrast to what happened with the earlier examples.

So, when we get round to stating the rules for forming questions in English (which I won't attempt here), we'll have to complicate those rules by adding a rider: 'except in cases like (2.22), in which you can't form a question at all'. But what exactly *are* the 'cases like (2.22)'? What's special and different about them?

This is the question that John Ross succeeded in answering in 1967. I'll give you his rule, but once again you may find it bewildering:

(2.23) A complex noun phrase is an island.

Again some mysterious terms, and again the same problem in explaining them. To explain what a *complex noun phrase* is, I'd first have to explain what a *noun phrase* is; to do that, I'd first have to explain what a *noun* is and what a *phrase* is; to explain what an *island* is, I'd first have to explain what a *dependency* is; to explain what a dependency is, I'd first have to – well, you surely get the picture by now. Once again, the best I can do in plain English is to offer the following very crude and inadequate approximation to Ross's rule:

(2.24) You can't ask a question about something that's inside a relative clause.

If you know what a relative clause is (and this is another fairly traditional piece of technical terminology), then you can at least see that in (2.21) the phrase *a car* occurs inside one (specifically, *who arrived in a car*), and hence Ross's rule predicts that (2.22) must be ungrammatical. And if you don't know what a relative clause is, you'll just have to take my word for it that Ross's rule works: unfortunately, I simply don't have the space here to explain that much grammar.

My crude paraphrase in (2.24) doesn't really work very well, though. Look at another pair of examples:

(2.25) The rumour that John has stolen a car is completely untrue.
(2.26) *Which car is the rumour that John has stolen completely untrue?

As you can easily confirm, (2.26) is also grossly ungrammatical, but this time there is no relative clause in sight. The inclusion of this somewhat different case is the reason Ross's rule is formulated in terms of something called a *complex noun phrase*. Ross's rule works for cases like (2.26); my 'plain English' paraphrase doesn't.

And once again you *know* Ross's rule. You never get it wrong. You never ask an ungrammatical question like (2.22), and, if a foreign learner of English mistakenly did so, you would instantly spot the mistake. Again, this is not anybody's opinion, and there is no point in discussing whether we ought to allow questions like (2.22). They are prohibited by the rules of English grammar, and that is the end of it.

Langacker's rule (which is technically called the *Precede-and-Command Condition*) and Ross's rule (which is technically called the *Complex Noun Phrase Constraint*) are just two of the many rules which combine and interact to produce the complete grammar of English. All these rules are built into the language, and they can only be uncovered by patient and careful investigation of the sort which grammarians have practised for generations. Like others before and since, Langacker and Ross have made their contributions to the enterprise of describing the grammar of English, an enterprise which is far from complete even today. Perhaps a few of the younger readers of this book will one day also have rules of grammar named after them.

The categories of grammar

The grammar of any language is articulated in terms of a sizeable number of classes of items and forms: the **categories of grammar**. These categories are, moreover, of several different types. Here I have space only to introduce a representative sample of these categories. To begin with, the vocabulary of every language contains many tens of thousands of words. And once again I mean *every* language: it is simply not true that some human speech communities make do with a few hundred words supplemented by grunts and gestures – this curious belief, which pops up from time to time, is merely the result of misunderstanding, ignorance and prejudice.

However, nearly all the words in any one language fall into a small number of categories, the **lexical categories**, also called *word classes* or *parts of speech*. The words in each category exhibit rather similar grammatical behaviour, while words in different categories behave quite differently. How many lexical categories are there? Well, for English, about fifteen; the precise number is still being debated. Among these are such traditional categories as *noun*, *verb*, *adjective* and *preposition*, identified by the Greek grammarians thousands of years ago, as well as a few more identified only in the twentieth century, such as *complementizer* (like *whether*) and *determiner* (like *the* and *this*).

How can we tell to which category a particular word belongs? Traditional grammarians often tried to answer this question in terms of the meanings of words, and produced attempted definitions like 'a noun is the name of a person, place or thing' and 'an adjective is a word that denotes a quality'. But such definitions are hopelessly

35

inadequate. According to the definition, the word *red*, which is surely the name of a colour, must therefore be a noun. Yet, in a typical sentence like *Lisa bought a red skirt*, *red* is not a noun but an adjective. All definitions based on meaning run into similar problems, because lexical categories are not really categories based on meaning at all: rather, they are grammatical categories, and they must be defined in terms of their grammatical properties.

How can we do this? Here are a few suggestions for defining the class of nouns. First, nouns have certain **distributional** properties: they occur in certain positions in sentences but not in other positions. Consider the following 'frames':

(2.27) The ___ was nice.
(2.28) The ___ were nice.

Any word which can appear in one of these blanks to make a good sentence must be a noun, because the grammar of English permits nouns, and only nouns, to appear in such positions. Thus, *wine*, *grass*, *book*, *destruction*, *development* and *opening* can all appear in the first, while *books*, *scissors*, *police*, *sheep* and *phenomena* can all appear in the second: hence all of these words are nouns. (The reason I need two frames is that the category of nouns is intersected by another category, discussed below.) On the other hand, such words as *happy*, *arrive*, *with*, *the*, *slowly* and *therefore* cannot appear in either blank, and hence these words are not nouns.

Second, nouns have certain **inflectional** properties: that is, they change their forms in certain ways for grammatical purposes within sentences. In English, the only important inflectional variation exhibited by nouns is that between the two forms called *singular* and *plural*. The singular and plural forms of a few English nouns are *dog/dogs*, *box/boxes*, *library/libraries*, *child/children*, *radius/radii* and *person/people*. Note that it is the singular forms which fit into (2.27), while the plural forms fit into (2.28).

Interestingly, not all English nouns show the singular/plural distinction. The nouns *wheat*, *furniture* and *spaghetti*, for example, have only a singular form, while *oats*, *police*, *pants* and *scissors* have only a plural form. Nevertheless, all these words behave like nouns in other respects, and hence they are nouns, even if slightly unusual ones.

Third, nouns have certain **derivational** properties: that is, they can take certain prefixes and suffixes in order to derive other words, often words belonging to different lexical categories. Many nouns, for example, take the suffix *-like* to derive adjectives: *dog/doglike*, *box/boxlike*, *child/childlike*, and perhaps even *spaghetti/spaghettilike*. (This last is not a word you see every day, but it sounds fine to me.) On the other hand, the prefix *un-*, which attaches itself happily to adjectives (*happy/unhappy*; *interesting/uninteresting*), categorically refuses to go onto nouns: *dog/*undog, joy/*unjoy, oats/*unoats, destruction/*undestruction*. (As always, the asterisk indicates a non-existent or impossible form.)

Grammarians have been largely successful in identifying the distinctive properties of each of the fifteen or so lexical categories in English, and the remaining disagreements are only about some minor matters of detail. One interesting finding has been that a few English words don't belong to any category at all. Such words as *please*, *not* and the 'infinitival' *to* found in *I want to be alone* all exhibit unique grammatical behaviour: each of them behaves quite differently from every other word in the language, and hence these words cannot be assigned to any lexical category. Many traditional grammarians had the bad habit of calling most of these special words 'adverbs', but that's just because they used 'adverb' as a dustbin category for all the words they didn't know what to do with.

The category of number

Above I remarked that the category of nouns in English is intersected by a second category. This second category is called **number**. Number is another important category in English, but it's not a lexical category. Rather, it's a different sort of category that cuts across certain lexical categories and affects their forms in particular sentences. Most obviously, number affects nouns. As we saw above, most nouns in English have two forms, a singular and a plural, though some have only one or the other. As is well known, the choice between the two forms is usually determined by whether we are talking about one object or more than one object:

(2.29) The dog is hungry.
(2.30) The dogs are hungry.

In (2.29), there is clearly only one canine animal under discussion, while in (2.30) there are at least two, and possibly many more than two. Things are not always so straightforward, however:

(2.31) The dog is closely related to the wolf.

In the most obvious reading of (2.31), we are not talking about any single dog, but about *all* dogs – and yet we use a singular form. Thus the singular form is obligatory in talking about one individual, and optional when talking about all individuals, but usually impossible when talking about any number of individuals greater than one but fewer than all. Curious, eh?

In fact, number in English shows quite a few peculiarities. By any objective standard, the word *scissors* or the word *pants* would appear unmistakably to denote a single object, and yet these words are strictly plural: they have no singular form at all:

(2.32) *This scissor(s) is very sharp.
(2.33) *This pant(s) is nearly dry.

This is unexpected. The word *bra*, for example, has the ordinary singular and plural forms. Is there any reason why *bra* should be singular but *pants* plural? So far as I can see, there is no sensible reason for this: it's just a curious idiosyncrasy of the grammar of English. The opposite idiosyncrasy is exhibited by the word *furniture*: when you talk about 'the furniture in the lounge', you almost certainly have several entirely distinct objects in mind, and yet the word *furniture* is strictly singular:

(2.34) *These furniture(s) are rather nice.

What about grain? When you look at a field of grain, are you looking at one object or at quite a lot of objects? Here, the answer is not obvious, and it's far from clear that the distinction between one object and more than one object is of any relevance to grain. But the grammar of English forces us to choose either a singular form or a plural form for every noun we use, with the result that we make arbitrary choices: the word *wheat* is singular (and has no plural), while *oats* is plural (and has no singular). Every English noun must always appear either as a singular or as a plural, and there is no possibility of avoiding the choice.

This is what typically happens with grammatical categories like number, which affect the forms of certain words. Once the category is in the language, every relevant word is forced to appear in one or another of the available forms. There is no possibility of avoiding the choice, even when it appears to be irrelevant.

Is the category of number universal? No, it is not. Most other European languages have a system very similar to that of English, with nouns typically distinguishing singular and plural forms. (There are, of course, a few minor differences. The French word for *pants* has both singular and plural forms; the Spanish words for *asparagus* and *spinach* have both singular and plural forms; the Basque word for *cabbage* has only a plural form, and the Basque word for *grape*(*s*) has only a singular form.)

Many languages, however, lack the category of number altogether, at least in nouns. Chinese and Japanese, for example, do not distinguish singular and plural forms of nouns, and Malay (the chief language of Malaysia) does not normally do so. In such languages, distinctions of number are simply not part of the grammar; when they are important, they must be expressed by using suitable words, such as *one*, *two* or *many*.

Other languages have more elaborate number distinctions than English. Arabic, for example, has a three-way number distinction in nouns: *malikun* 'king', *malikani* 'two kings', *malikuna* '(three or more) kings'; the second form is called the **dual**. The Pacific language Larike goes one step further by adding to this a **trial**, though only in pronouns, not in nouns: *mane* 'he' or 'she', *matua* 'they two', *matidu* 'they three', *mati* 'they (four or more)'. The East African language Tigre has a different three-way distinction for nouns, adding to the singular and plural a **paucal** or 'little plural': *färäs* 'horse', *ʔäfras* 'a few horses', *ʔäfresam* 'horses'. (*ʔ* in these words represents a glottal stop.) Languages are free to make any grammatical distinctions of number they like, including none at all, but, once a distinction is built

39

into the grammar, the distinctions between number forms must be rigorously observed.

Gender

Of all the grammatical categories which are important in human languages, one of the strangest is **gender**. Gender is also one of the most misunderstood categories, and I shall try to clarify the meaning of this term a little.

In a language with gender (and only a minority of languages have it), all the nouns are divided up into two or more classes, called gender classes, with noticeable differences in the grammatical behaviour of the nouns in each class.

French, for example, has two gender classes, traditionally called *masculine* and *feminine* (though these names are somewhat misleading). The words in the two classes differ grammatically in several ways. For example, the word for *the* with a singular masculine noun is *le*, while for a feminine noun it's *la*. Thus, 'the book' is *le livre*, since *livre* 'book' is masculine, while 'the table' is *la table*, since *table* 'table' is feminine. Every noun in the language is assigned to one or the other of these two genders: hence *le chien* 'the dog', *le mot* 'the word', *le bifteck* 'the steak', and *le mystère* 'the mystery', but *la maison* 'the house', *la voiture* 'the car', *la moutarde* 'the mustard', and *la découverte* 'the discovery'.

The traditional names of the genders are given because most nouns denoting males fall into the *le* gender and most nouns denoting females into the *la* gender: hence *homme* 'man', *taureau* 'bull' and *maître* 'master' are masculine, while *femme* 'woman', *vache* 'cow' and *maîtresse* 'mistress' are feminine. But the matchup is not perfect: *sentinelle* 'sentry' is feminine, even though most sentries are men, and *contralto* 'contralto' is masculine, even though all contraltos are women. In any case, the vast majority of nouns in French do not denote either males or females, and these are simply assigned to one gender or the other on an arbitrary basis – arbitrary, that is, as far as their meanings are concerned. There is nothing particularly masculine about books or words or mysteries, and nothing particularly feminine about cars or mustard or discoveries.

In other words – and this is a key point – there is no particular connection between gender and sex. Sex is a matter of biology, while gender is a matter of grammar, and there is no earthly reason why sex should be involved in gender distinctions. In French, it is involved, but only in a somewhat weak and inconsistent way: the gender of most nouns has nothing at all to do with sex.

In many gender languages, gender shows no connection with sex, and sometimes little or no connection with meaning at all. In the African language Swahili, for example, there are eight gender classes. Most words denoting human beings, of either sex, belong to the same gender class, sometimes called gender class number one, which also includes most words for animals. A second gender class contains many words for large things, and a third class many words for small things. After this, though, the assignment of gender in Swahili becomes rather arbitrary and unpredictable. Gender in Swahili correlates only feebly with meaning and not at all with sex.

The North American language Navaho has ten genders. In Navaho, gender is strongly predictable from meaning, but sex again plays no part. There is one gender for nouns denoting human beings, another for liquids, a third for round things (like stones and balls), a fourth for long stiff things (like pencils and ski poles), a fifth for long floppy things (like ropes and belts) and so on.

A non-European language in which sex does correlate with gender is the Australian language Dyirbal. The Dyirbal gender system is remarkable and famous, and we shall briefly look at it here. Dyirbal has four gender classes, and gender assignment is largely predictable, but *only* with certain extra information. Here is a summary of the groups of words belonging to each of the four Dyirbal genders:

Gender 1	*Gender 2*
men	women
kangaroos	bandicoots
possums	dogs
bats	platypus, echidna
most snakes	dangerous snakes
most fishes	dangerous fishes
certain birds	most birds

most insects

fireflies, crickets
scorpions
some stinging insects
all words connected with fire
all words connected with water

moon
storms, rainbow
boomerangs
hunting spears
etc.

sun, stars

shields
fighting spears
dangerous plants
etc.

Gender 3
all trees and plants with
edible parts

Gender 4
parts of the body
meat
bees and honey
wind
digging sticks
trees and plants neither edible
    nor harmful
mud, stones
noises, language
etc.

As in French, the different gender classes of Dyirbal require different words for *the*, but this time there are four of them: *bayi* for Gender 1, *balan* for 2, *balam* for 3, and *bala* for 4.

The basic rules for gender assignment in Dyirbal work approximately as follows:

1 Words pertaining to men or to non-human creatures go into Gender 1.
2 Words pertaining to women, to fire, to water or to fighting go into Gender 2.
3 Words pertaining to edible plants go into Gender 3.
4 All other words go into Gender 4.

However, these basic rules are disturbed by several special rules, which take priority:

5   Any word that denotes something connected in myths with men
     or with women goes into Gender 1 or Gender 2, respectively.
6   Any word denoting something dangerous goes into Gender 2.
7   Any word denoting something of unique importance in Dyirbal
     society goes into some unexpected gender.

Let's clarify the gender listings above by reference to these rules. Most words in Gender 1 relate to men or to non-human creatures, by Rule 1. Boomerangs and hunting spears are used in hunting, which is performed only by men, and hence are also here. The moon, storms and rainbows are regarded as men in Dyirbal myths, and hence, by Rule 5, these words are also in Gender 1. Gender 2 includes words for women, fire, water and fighting, by Rule 2. But all words denoting dangerous items go into Gender 2 by Rule 6, even if they would otherwise be in a different gender – hence, words for poisonous snakes, nettles, stinging grubs, and the like all belong here. In myths, birds are mostly regarded as the spirits of women, and so bird names mostly belong to Gender 2 by Rule 5; a few birds, however, are mythically men and these names are in Gender 1. The sun is mythically female, and both it and the stars are fiery anyway, so here they are in Gender 2. It is not known why bandicoots, dogs, platypus and echidna are in Gender 2; either they have unidentified mythical associations, or else these assignments are just arbitrary and contrary to the usual rules, like the French words for 'sentry' and 'contralto'. Gender 3 is reserved for edible plants, and Gender 4 is the 'residue' class containing all the words that don't fit into any of the first three classes. Bees and honey are in Gender 4 by Rule 7, because honey, the only sweet food and the source of the only drink other than water, is of unique importance in Dyirbal society. In this fascinating system, gender assignment is thus far more predictable than in French or Swahili, but the rules are nonetheless a little mysterious.

Finally, what about English? Well, English has no grammatical gender. We do, of course, have some words that intrinsically denote males, such as *bull* and *duke*, and others that denote females, such as *cow* and *duchess*. And among our pronouns we have a distinction among *he* (applied to males), *she* (applied to females) and *it* (applied to non-humans and sometimes to infants). But that's it. Unlike French or Swahili or Dyirbal, English does not divide its nouns up into classes requiring different grammatical behaviour. Like all languages, English has certain devices for indicating the sometimes important distinctions of sex, but English has no gender.

Further reading

A useful introductory book on grammar is Palmer (1984) – though, if you're not at all familiar with the terminology of traditional grammar, it would be wise to start with Crystal (1988a). Fabb (1994) is an elementary introduction to grammatical theory; a more substantial introduction to grammar is Brown and Miller (1991). An excellent place to read about grammatical categories is Lyons (1971, Ch. 7). Gender is covered in detail in Corbett (1991). The Dyirbal language is described in Dixon (1972); all my information comes from this book.

Chapter 3

Language and meaning

Most people, when asked what language is for, reply that the function of language is to express and communicate meanings. Certainly this ability to express meanings is an indispensable aspect of language. Most of the other functions of language would scarcely be available to us if our utterances were not capable of carrying meanings. But what sort of thing *is* a meaning? How do we recognize a meaning when we see one?

This is not a simple question. Indeed, there is perhaps no other question touching on language to which the answer is less obvious or more controversial. The study of meaning is called **semantics**, and semantics has for generations been the branch of linguistics in which, more than any other, it has often seemed maddeningly difficult to make any progress at all. Very often, semanticists have not even agreed about which questions ought to be asked, let alone about what the answers might be. In the 1940s and 1950s, many linguists in the USA became so

exasperated with the whole messy business of semantics that they simply defined the subject of linguistics as one excluding semantics, on the ground that the study of meaning was just too much of a swamp to be examined profitably with linguistic techniques. Fortunately, this discouraged view has not prevailed, and semantics is today one of the liveliest areas in all of linguistics. But the questions are still very hard. In this chapter we'll be looking at just a few of the ways meanings are expressed in language.

The difficulty of defining words

The meaning of a sentence clearly depends upon at least two other things: the meanings of the words in the sentence, and the grammatical structure of the sentence. Consider the following examples:

(3.1) The dog bit the milkman.
(3.2) The dog bit the postman.
(3.3) The dog is biting the postman.
(3.4) The postman bit the dog.

The first two examples have identical grammatical structures, but they contain different words, and hence they have different meanings. The second and third examples contain more or less the same words, but they clearly have different grammatical structures, and hence they too have different meanings. Finally, examples (3.2) and (3.4) have identical grammatical structures, and they contain exactly the same words, but they still have very different meanings, because the words have been embedded into the grammatical structure in different ways.

So, if we want to know what the meaning of a sentence is, it appears that we need to know at least two things: we need to know what all the words mean, and we need to understand every detail of the grammatical structure. Is that all we need to know? Some people would say that it is. The view that this is all we need to know in order to understand the meaning of a sentence has been very influential in semantics, and it rejoices in a mouth-filling name: it is called **Frege's Principle of Compositionality**, after the German philosopher who first proposed it.

As we shall see later in this chapter, things may not be so simple as Frege's principle would suggest. Meanwhile, though, let us assume that the grammarians who we left in Chapter 2 are doing a good job explaining the grammar, and let us turn to the problem of explaining what the words mean.

The study of word meanings is called **lexical semantics**. Lexical semantics deals, not just with the meanings of individual words, but also with the way in which the meanings of different words are related. But we have to start somewhere, so let me ask a simple question: what is the meaning of the word *dog*?

I'll clarify this question a bit. Imagine that the first Martian has just landed on earth. He's managed to learn a bit of English by listening to radio broadcasts from earth, but he's never seen a dog. In fact, he's never heard the word before, and now he wants you to give him a perfect definition. With your definition, he's going to go strolling around the planet, and, every time he comes across something new, he's going to consult your definition in order to find out if he's looking at a dog or not. In every single case, without exception, he wants your definition to give him the right result. If your definition fails him even once, he's going to be *very* annoyed. Take a couple of minutes now and write down your definition of a dog.

Perhaps, before we go further, you'd like to compare your definition with the one found in a good dictionary. Here is the definition from the *Collins English Dictionary* (I omit some additional senses which are not relevant here):

> **dog** *n.* **1.** a domesticated canine mammal, *Canis familiaris*, occurring in many breeds that show a great variety in size and form. **2.** any other carnivore of the family *Canidae*, such as the dingo and coyote.

Very likely your definition is quite different from this one, and we'll look at yours in a minute. For the moment, let's assume our Martian has taken the dictionary definition with him.

His first problem is that the dictionary gives two different meanings for *dog*. This is obviously going to make life difficult, so let's tell him to ignore the second one – when you wrote your definition, you probably weren't thinking about dingos and coyotes anyway.

So off goes our Martian, and before long he stumbles across something unfamiliar. Is it a dog or not? He consults the definition. First, he checks to see if he's looking at a mammal. This is not so easy. Remember, many biologists at first refused to believe that the platypus was a mammal: it has webbed feet and lays eggs, not very typical mammalian characteristics. But we'll assume our Martian is a good zoologist, and he soon satisfies himself that he is indeed looking at a mammal.

Next question: is it a canine mammal? This question is impossible to answer, for *canine* is simply another word for *dog*. If you know it's a dog, then you know it's a canine, but, if you don't know whether it's a dog, asking whether it's a canine is no help at all.

All right, then: is it domesticated? How is our Martian going to work this out? Maybe it has a collar – but having a collar certainly isn't part of anybody's definition of a dog, and anyway lots of cats wear collars, not to mention a very large number of human beings. Suppose the thing in front of our Martian is standing there growling in a menacing manner. Suppose, in fact, that it's hurling itself berserkly against a chain fence and generally intimating that it is eager to rip his Martian throat out. Is it still possibly domesticated? Does this behaviour disqualify it from being a dog?

Nervously, our Martian consults the rest of the definition. Does the thing in front of him occur in many breeds of different sizes and forms? Not obviously – the thing in front of him only seems to have one size and one form. Even if he comes across some other things that look different from the one now in front of him, how is he going to know if they're all different breeds of dog if he can't tell whether any one of them is a dog to begin with?

We're not making a lot of progress here. Maybe it's time we turned to your definition. What have you written? Suppose you've written something like this:

> A dog is a four-legged animal, covered in thick fur, with an elongated snout, long ears, claws on its feet, and a tail. It eats meat, chases smaller animals, and utters a distinctive barking

noise. If raised from infancy by humans, it will remain with those humans.

Is our Martian going to find this definition more satisfactory than the dictionary's effort? Well, this is a good attempt, but there are still some serious problems. What about that fur? If an animal has no fur on its nose, on its feet, inside its ears, and in a few other places, is it still 'covered in fur'? If it's lost all its fur through illness, does that mean it can't be a dog? And how long do ears have to be to count as 'long ears'? Four inches? Six inches? Can an animal miss being a dog because its ears are slightly too short? And the elongated snout? Bulldogs and pekineses certainly don't have elongated snouts, yet we still count them as dogs.

And what is a barking noise, anyway? We apply the term *bark* to everything from the deep woof of a bloodhound to the shrill yapping of a lap dog. How do we know these are all barks? In practice, we probably decide that a noise is a bark because we recognize that it's being produced by a dog – but this isn't going to help our Martian much.

Certain breeds of dog, such as the Mexican hairless, fail this definition because they have no fur – yet we still call them dogs. And some, like the basenji, cannot bark – but the basenji is a dog. Lots of dogs have no tail, but that doesn't stop them from being dogs. Little by little, this definition is beginning to come apart.

How about those dingos and coyotes mentioned by the dictionary, not to mention wolves, foxes, hyenas and jackals? Are these animals dogs? If not, why not? Where do they fall short of the definition? They all make various yelping noises that we might reasonably count as barking, and the fox's yelp, at least, commonly *is* called a bark. Wolves and possibly some of the others can be domesticated, and in fact dogs originated as domesticated wolves: even today, dogs can interbreed with wolves.

Come to think of it, the only part of our definition that doesn't apply straightforwardly to a cat is the barking noise. However, if you came across an unusual cat that could produce a dog-like yap, would that qualify the animal as a dog? Why not?

Is a dead dog still a dog? A stuffed dog prepared by a

taxidermist? How about a statue of a dog? A photograph of a dog? A painting of a dog? All these things would seem to fail our definition drastically, yet we still unhesitatingly apply the word *dog* to every one of them. Even Snoopy the cartoon beagle is a dog – but he's just a collection of inky lines on paper.

This is all getting a bit depressing, and our Martian is certainly not going to be satisfied. 'How can you go around using the word *dog* so happily', he asks in bewilderment, 'when you obviously don't know what it means?'

But, of course, we *do* know what the word means. If somebody says to you 'There's a strange dog in the garden', you know at once what to expect, and you won't be expecting a coyote or a cat. In practice, we all know the meaning of the word, even if we can't define it. This situation is a little reminiscent of what we encountered in Chapter 2: we all know the rules of English grammar, even though we can't state them. We run into the same problem with almost every other word we try to define.

It's only for a small minority of words that we can give definitions without these fuzzy edges. Until recently, the *metre* was officially defined as the distance between two particular scratches on a particular metal bar kept in a particular vault in Paris, and, if you wanted to know if your metre stick was a metre long or not, all you had to do was to take it to Paris and lay it alongside that bar. That works pretty well for *metre*, but it wouldn't work for most other words: we could hardly keep a standard dog in a vault to compare against candidate dogs, or a standard chair, or a standard smile.

How, then, do we manage to use all these words so effortlessly if we can't define them? This is not a simple question, and both linguists and psychologists have pondered it at length. One plausible suggestion is the **stereotype** theory. The idea here is that we carry in our heads, as a result of our experience, a picture of a stereotypical dog. When we encounter a candidate dog, we compare it with our mental stereotype to see if the match is good enough. If it is, we decide we're looking at a dog; if it's not, we decide otherwise. In this approach, then, probably no single criterion is decisive, and we can accept a dog with no fur, or a dog that can't bark, as long as enough other features match.

Fine, and very plausible, but how many stereotypical dog features can be missing before we decide we're not looking at a dog? In other words, how do stereotypes allow us to cope with borderline cases? We have a potentially devastating problem here, but we are rescued by something which is not a fact about language at all: the way the world is arranged. In practice, almost every object we come across is either pretty clearly a dog or pretty clearly not a dog. That is, either it matches our stereotype rather well, or it doesn't match well at all. It's not just cats and toasters that fail to exhibit an adequate number of doggy characteristics: even foxes and coyotes fail to do so. Wolves provide the toughest test, but an important part of our doggy stereotype seems to be that dogs are found with or near people, whereas wolves, when we encounter them at all, generally turn up in remote areas, well away from people and mostly having nothing to do with them.

There is, however, at least one major area in which it *is* absolutely vital to decide whether a particular word is appropriate or not: the law. You have to pay tax on your income, but what is income? Are tips income? Are gifts income? Are your poker winnings income? If you find some money in the street, is that income? Somebody has to give definitive answers to these questions, so that you know how much tax to pay. Lawyers spend much of their time arguing over questions like these, and judges and juries are called upon to give rulings one way or the other. Whereas most of us, most of the time, never worry about the edges of our words, the law is concerned with little else.

Word meanings and the structure of the vocabulary

Words do not have meanings in isolation. In general, the meaning of a word is related to the meanings of other words in ways that may be simple or complex. So, for example, *young* is more closely related to *old* than it is to *lazy*. Likewise, *rose* is related in one way to *flower*, in another way to *lilac*, and in a third way to *red*. Much of the business of lexical semantics lies in clarifying these relationships in meaning.

One obvious way for words to be related in meaning is

synonymy: the case in which they have identical meanings. But *are* there any words which have exactly the same meaning? Yes and no. Consider *pail* and *bucket*. Anything which can be called a pail can also be called a bucket, and vice versa, so to that extent they are synonymous. However, these words are not interchangeable. Which you use depends on where you come from. Broadly speaking, in England, in Wales, and in the southern USA *bucket* is normal, the *unmarked* word, and *pail* is rustic, while in Scotland and in the northern USA *pail* is normal and *bucket* is rustic.

That little complication aside, the point here is that, even when two words can be applied to exactly the same range of objects or events, they often have different associations. The concert musician Anne-Sophie Mutter plays a *violin*, while a square-dance caller plays a *fiddle*, but the instrument is the same (except probably in price and quality). The words *big* and *large* seem to be synonymous, but think of all those expressions in which only *big* is possible: *She got her big break in London, and now she's a big noise at the BBC and she's making big money.*

Are these associations part of the meanings of words? That depends on what you're trying to do. If you're only interested in deciding which objects or phenomena a word can possibly refer to, you can forget the associations and declare that *violin* and *fiddle* are truly synonyms. But, if you're interested in the proper use of words in context, the associations are important. A foreign learner of English who talks solemnly about a fiddle concerto is not going to achieve the desired effect.

Another familiar relation in meaning is **antonymy**. Antonyms are words which have opposite meanings. That sounds simple enough, but, as usual, things are more complicated than they might at first appear. Pairs of antonyms like *hot* and *cold*, *dead* and *alive*, *married* and *single*, *open* and *shut* are not all related in the same way. Take a look at the following sentences, and try to decide whether each one might be a reasonable thing to say or not. To avoid irrelevant complications, assume that all the names refer to adult human beings.

(3.5)   This water is neither hot nor cold.
(3.6)   This table is neither clean nor dirty.

(3.7)   That door is neither open nor shut.
(3.8)   Janet is neither married nor single.
(3.9)   My friend Sandy is neither male nor female.
(3.10) Your statement is neither true nor false.
(3.11) Her results are neither good nor bad.

How do you feel about these? I can tell you that the only ones that everybody seems to agree on are the first one and the last one: all the others are controversial. Everyone seems happy to accept a range of possibilities lying between *hot* and *cold*, or between *good* and *bad*: these are what we call **gradable antonyms**. Some people feel the same about *clean* and *dirty*, but others disagree: they maintain adamantly that anything that isn't clean must be dirty, with no middle ground. For such speakers, *clean* and *dirty* are **binary antonyms**, which means that the two words are incompatible and that, between them, they exhaust all the possibilities. Most people find that *true* or *false*, or *dead* and *alive*, are better examples of binary antonyms, but here too there is disagreement. Are these statements true or false: *Italy is shaped like a boot*; *It's sixty miles from London to Brighton*; *It'll probably rain tomorrow*?

The case of *married* and *single* is particularly interesting. Some people insist that any adult is necessarily either married or single, and will not listen to any arguments for any other view. Others are equally sure that *married* and *single* are just two of a number of possibilities, including *engaged*, *attached*, *living with someone*, *separated*, *divorced*, *widowed*, and possibly others. Indeed, a discussion on this point can become quite heated.

The gradable antonyms have another property which, when you think about it, is rather remarkable. Suppose our Martian, having given up on dogs, comes back to you and asks 'What temperature does something have to be at in order to be *hot*?' There is, of course, no answer to this, except perhaps 'Well, it all depends.' A temperature of 95°C (near boiling) is certainly hot if we're talking about bath water, but an oven at this temperature is not remotely hot. Whereas 30°C represents a hot July day in London, it's a cool one in Dallas. And the sun, with a surface temperature of around 6,000°C, is considered by astronomers to be a rather cool star. What it all depends on, then, is our expectations. We describe bath water or ovens as hot if they have temperatures near the upper end of our expectations for bath water or ovens, and hence the word *hot* has no absolute meaning, nor has any other gradable word like *good* or *big*. We shift effortlessly between *hot coffee* and *hot day*, between *big butterfly*, *big dog*, *big truck* and *big island*, and between *good wine*, *good news*, *good doctor* and *good weather*, usually without even noticing what we're doing. This is fascinating and far from trivial. The scientists and engineers trying to develop what is called *artificial intelligence* find it maddeningly difficult to program their computers to use words in such a shifty way.

Another type of relation is that illustrated by *rose* and *flower*. Anything which is a rose is necessarily also a flower, but the converse is not true: a flower might be a rose, but it might be a daffodil or a tiger lily. We say that *rose* is a **hyponym** of *flower*, while *flower* is a **superordinate** of *rose*.

Hyponymy is commonplace, but not always straightforward. *Rose* is certainly a hyponym of *flower*, but is *flower* a hyponym of *plant*? Or is a flower only a part of a plant? If I were to ask you for some hyponyms of *container*, you might come up with *box*, *jar* or *bag*. But what about *envelope*, *shrink-wrapping*, *mailbox* or *pocket*? Do these words denote containers or not? If not, why not? They all contain things, so where do they fall short of being containers?

In fact, it is rather a matter of hit or miss whether we even have a superordinate word for a section of our vocabulary. We happen to have the word *tree* for any large, woody plant, even though trees do not constitute a single group in the taxonomic classification of plants used by botanists. Some other languages have no such word: some Australian languages, for example, have no equivalent to *tree*, but only names for particular kinds of tree. On the other hand, some other languages have a single superordinate term meaning 'flying creature', applied to any bird, bat or insect which can fly – but English has no equivalent. (Amusingly, linguistically ignorant Europeans have sometimes condemned the speakers of supposedly 'primitive' non-European languages on *both* these counts: the non-Europeans are condemned for not having a word like *tree* on the ground that they fail to draw obvious generalizations, and condemned also for having a word meaning 'flying creature' on the ground that they fail to make obvious distinctions. I hope it is obvious to readers of this book that condemning people for being different from Europeans, for linguistic or other reasons, is so much racist nonsense.)

In English it is often a matter of debate whether particular words are hyponyms of a generic term or not. The same is true of most other languages, but the languages of Australia offer us a remarkable opportunity to find out very explicitly which words are hyponyms. Every Australian language has a special way of speaking called an **avoidance style** which must be used in the presence of certain relatives. These relatives always include a man's mother-in-law, and hence avoidance styles are often called *mother-in-law language*. The avoidance style differs from everyday speech only in its vocabulary: there are different words for things. Importantly, the number of words in the avoidance style is typically much smaller than the number of words in the everyday style, and the avoidance style is therefore rich in generic terms: one generic term in the avoidance style does duty for a number of different words in the everyday style. Consequently, we have direct evidence about lexical semantics: all those everyday words which are rendered by a single term in the avoidance style are presumably regarded by speakers as hyponyms of some superordinate notion, even if the everyday language does not provide a suitable superordinate term. I shall illustrate this arrangement with data from Dyirbal, an Australian language with a particularly well-developed avoidance style.

Everyday Dyirbal has no generic term for lizards, but only specific names for particular lizards: *banggarra* 'blue-tongue lizard', *biyu* 'frilled lizard', *buynyjul* 'red-bellied lizard', *gaguju* 'water skink', *bajirri* 'water goanna', and so on. The avoidance style has only a single term for all of these, *jijan*, and so we may conclude that Dyirbal-speakers regard all these terms as hyponyms of a super-ordinate, even though the everyday style does not actually have a superordinate term.

Occasionally there are uncertainties or disagreements. It is recorded that a Dyirbal couple disagreed about how to render the everyday word *darrbin* 'shake [something] off a blanket': the man preferred the avoidance term *bubaman* 'set in motion in a trajectory

55

while holding on' (the blanket is held on to), while his wife preferred *nayngun* 'set in motion in a trajectory while letting go' (the stuff on the blanket is flying off). In the majority of cases, though, there is no such choice, and the Australian mother-in-law styles present us with a fascinating and unique direct view of the way in which speakers organize their words in terms of meanings.

Meaning and grammar

So far I've been treating grammar and meaning as two entirely distinct aspects of language, and very often they are distinct. In other cases, though, they are intimately bound up together. We saw some examples of that in Chapter 2, when I talked about the grammatical categories of number and gender. Such categories represent cases in which certain aspects of meaning are built into the grammar of a language. Here I want to discuss another grammatical category, one whose close connection with meaning is obvious, even if not so easy to describe. That category is *tense*.

Tense is the grammaticalization of time, but it is important to realize that tense and time are two quite different things. To begin with, time is not an aspect of language at all, but an aspect of physics and psychology. We are all aware of the passage of time, and we find it convenient to chop up the flow of time into the chunks we call *past*, *present* and *future*. In fact, we can chop up time into much finer segments than these three, if we want to. We can distinguish the recent past from the remote past, or the near future from the distant future. We can distinguish *a few moments ago* from *earlier today*, *yesterday* from *the day before yesterday*, *last week* from *last month* and *last year*. There is absolutely no limit to the time distinctions we can make: *127 years ago* is different from *128 years ago*. But notice that all these distinctions are made simply by using suitable words, or suitable collections of words. So far, these distinctions have nothing to do with the grammar of English.

However, it is perfectly possible for a language to build some of these time distinctions into its grammar. Not all of them, of course: there are infinitely many distinctions of time. But a few of the major distinctions can be embedded firmly in the grammar of a language, and a language that does this has the category of *tense* in its grammar.

Like many other languages, English does this by marking tense distinctions on verbs. English verbs show a systematic tense distinction: *love* versus *loved*, *go* versus *went*, *do* versus *did*. The way our verbs mark tense is often somewhat irregular, but that doesn't matter. The connection between tense and time is, at first glance, fairly clear: *I love her* means now, but *I loved her* means in the past.

It may surprise you to learn that not all languages do this: some languages do not have tense. Chinese is one such. There is nothing in Chinese comparable to the *go/went* distinction in English. A Chinese speaker must always express distinctions of time, when necessary, by adding suitable time words to the sentence: *I go now*, *I go yesterday*, *I go tomorrow*, *I go in ten minutes*, *I go twenty years ago*. This works just fine, and Chinese speakers never miss the tense distinctions they haven't got.

Lots of languages, though, do have tense. Turkish, for example, has three tenses: past (*gittim* 'I went'), present (*gidiyorum* 'I'm going') and future (*gideceğim* 'I'll go'). This is a common system, but not the only one possible. Many languages have only two tenses, but tense systems can be considerably more elaborate. The West African language Bamileke-Dschang reportedly has no fewer than eleven tenses; these represent five different degrees of remoteness in the past and five degrees of remoteness in the future, as well as a present tense. Speakers of a language making such fine distinctions, or indeed speakers of any language with tense, do not have a choice as to which tense to use: they must use the tense form that represents the appropriate point in time. This is what I mean by saying that tense is a grammaticalization of time.

Tense is most often marked on verbs, but not always. The California language Hupa has tense-marking on nouns. Thus, for example, the word for 'house' has three tenses: a present tense *xonta* ('house which now exists'), a past tense *xontaneen* ('house which is now in ruins') and a future tense *xontate* ('house which is not built yet'). English, of course, has nothing like this, and we have to use different words to achieve the same effect: one might consider, for example, that *ex-wife* is the 'past tense' of *wife*, while *fiancée* is its 'future tense'!

Speaking of English, how many tenses does our language have? It is possible that you may find the answer surprising: English has only two tenses. These are traditionally called the *past tense* and the *present tense*, though *non-past tense* would be a better name for the second one. English has no future tense. Of course, we have many ways of talking about future time, but the forms we use to do this are all 'present tense' (non-past tense); these various forms allow us to express a wide range of subtly different attitudes toward future events, but none of them can properly be called a future tense. Here is a sample of the forms we use for talking about future time; in each case, I have set the present-tense form side by side with its corresponding past-tense form (except for the two unusual ones which have no past-tense counterparts).

(3.12) (a) She goes to London tomorrow.
      (b) She went to London yesterday.

(3.13) (a) She's going to London tomorrow.
      (b) She was going to London tomorrow.

(3.14) (a) She's going to go to London tomorrow.
      (b) She was going to go to London tomorrow.

(3.15) (a) She has to go to London tomorrow.
      (b) She had to go to London yesterday.

(3.16)   She must go to London tomorrow.

(3.17) (a) She will go to London tomorrow.
      (b) She would go to London tomorrow.

(3.18) (a) She shall go to London tomorrow.
      (b) She should go to London tomorrow.

(3.19) (a) She'll be going to London tomorrow.
      (b) She'd be going to London tomorrow.

(3.20) (a) She wants to go to London tomorrow.
      (b) She wanted to go to London tomorrow.

(3.21)   She ought to go to London tomorrow.

(Certain of the past-tense forms have specific meanings that do not allow the adverb *tomorrow*, and the relation in meaning between the present- and past-tense forms is not always straightforward, notably in (3.12).) If it's not clear that the (b) sentences are all in the past tense, observe what happens if you stick each of these after the introductions *Janet tells me that* ... and *Janet told me that* ... You should find that the second of these can only be followed by the (b) continuations, and not by the (a) ones, or at least that the (b) continuations sound much more natural; this is a standard test for past-tense forms in English.

You might like to amuse yourself by trying to work out just what the differences in meaning are among these various forms, but regrettably I don't have the space to consider that issue here.

Some traditional textbooks of English pick out just one of these forms, most often (3.17a), and arbitrarily label it the 'future tense'. This is wrong. The *will* form is no more a future tense than any of the others, and foreign learners of English who have been thus wrongly taught often wind up saying things like *What will you do tonight?* and *Oh, I shall go to a film*, or *When Janet will get here, we shall start*, utterances which I'm sure you will agree are not normal English. We say *What are you doing tonight?*, *Oh, I'm going to a film* and *When Janet gets here* ..., with no *will* or *shall*. In English, *will* and *shall* do not constitute a future tense; they are merely present-tense forms which, like *must*, *ought* and *have to*, express a particular view of a future event.

Even the past-tense forms in English are not confined to referring to past events. They have other uses, too. In examples like *It's time you went to bed* and *If I spoke better French, I could get a job in Paris*, the forms *went* and *spoke* are transparently past tense, but the going and speaking referred to are most definitely not in the past: the first lies in the immediate future, while the second lies in a hypothetical present or future. Such behaviour illustrates quite clearly why it is essential to distinguish between time (a non-linguistic concept) and tense (a grammatical category): the matchup is not necessarily perfect. (Of course, some traditional grammars refer to forms like my *went* and *spoke* as 'subjunctive' forms, but 'subjunctive' here is only a fancy label for a past-tense form that doesn't refer to past time, and we don't need it.)

And that, lest you begin to suspect that I'm sneaking too much tedious grammar into a chapter that's supposed to be about meaning, brings me to the main point of this discussion: while grammar certainly makes important contributions to the expression of meaning, grammar is not the same thing as meaning. Saying that Chinese does not have the grammatical category of tense (which is true) is a very different thing from saying that Chinese speakers cannot make distinctions of time (which is nonsense). Whether a language has eleven tenses, three tenses, two tenses or no tenses at all, its speakers have not the slightest difficulty in talking about any desired point in time, past, present or future. All languages can express things like *the Tuesday before last*, or *at 9.30 tomorrow morning*, or *in the year 1453*; they differ only in the amount of grammatical detail they glue onto the verb (or elsewhere) to help express these notions. Broadly speaking, anything that can be expressed in one language can be expressed in another language. This important observation is sometimes called the **Principle of Effability** (the fancy word *effable* just means 'expressible in words'). Most linguists are satisfied that this principle holds good, subject only to minor qualification for culture-bound references to shared experience. (For example, a discussion of Graham Gooch's batting technique would be rather difficult to express comprehensibly in Chinese, but then this would be equally difficult with an English-speaking audience ignorant of cricket – say in Chicago.) None the less, translation is not a trivial undertaking, and a few linguists have chosen to deny the Principle of Effability in favour of a dramatically different view of the relation between language and meaning. To this different view I now turn.

Meaning and the world

If you've ever tried to translate a text from one language into another, you will know that translation is far from easy. One big reason it's not easy is that words in different languages do not match up one to one. English, for example, makes a clear difference in meaning between *ape* and *monkey*, while French has only the single word *singe* to cover all these creatures. On the other hand, English has only *ball* to cover the six French words *boule*, *boulet*, *boulette*, *balle*, *pelote* and *ballon*, all of which have different meanings.

And these are simple cases. Much more typically, a stretch of meaning is just divided up by different languages into completely different and overlapping pieces. The three English words *road*, *street* and *way* cover about the same territory as the five French words *route*, *rue*, *chemin*, *voie* and *chaussée*, but no one of the English words exactly matches any one of the French words. The same is true of English *hard*, *harsh* and *rough* and French *dur*, *rêche*, *rude*, *âpre* and *rigoureux*; of English *large*, *big*, *great* and *grand* and French *grand* and *gros*; and so on *ad infinitum*.

English and French are both European languages, spoken in countries with similar societies and a very largely shared cultural tradition, but translating between them is still hard work. How much harder is it to translate between languages which are spoken by societies with utterly different backgrounds and traditions?

There is a view, a minority view but a prominent one none the less, that such translation can be almost impossible, and for a very interesting reason. This view was somewhat tentatively put forward by the great German–American linguist Edward Sapir, and was developed by Sapir's student Benjamin Lee Whorf; consequently, it is often known as the **Sapir–Whorf hypothesis**, though some prefer to call it the **linguistic relativity hypothesis**. The Sapir–Whorf hypothesis can be expressed in several ways and with varying degrees of robustness, but here is a common formulation of it: *the structure of our language in large measure affects the way we perceive the world*.

At first glance, this startling proposal might not seem entirely plausible. English-speakers have different words for apes and monkeys, while French speakers do not. Does it follow that English-speakers are better than the French at perceiving the difference between apes and monkeys? I very much doubt it: many English-speakers, in my experience, have little or no idea what distinguishes these two groups of animals and tend to use the words *ape* and *monkey* more or less interchangeably. But this is not quite the sort of thing that Whorf had in mind.

Whorf came to linguistics from a background as a fire insurance inspector. By his own account, what first attracted him to issues of language was petrol drums (gasoline drums). During his investigations, he discovered that workmen were usually scrupulously careful with full drums of petrol, but that they tended to take a very casual attitude to empty petrol drums. This is not objectively wise. If you toss a lighted match into a full petrol drum, the petrol just burns; if you toss one into an empty drum, the petrol vapours remaining in the drum will explode violently. Whorf concluded that there was something about the very word *empty* that was inducing such irrational behaviour on the part of the workmen.

Intrigued by such observations, Whorf took up the study of linguistics, and in particular the study of North American languages like Hopi, Nootka and Shawnee. What he found fascinated him. Hopi, for example, has a distinct future tense but no distinction between present and past tenses. However, Hopi has a verbal system which is very rich in other ways: verbs are inflected for such unfamiliar (to us) notions as duration and repetition. Very commonly, concepts which in English must be expressed by totally different verbs are expressed in Hopi by different forms of a single verb. Here is a sample:

róya 'it makes a turn'	*royáyata* 'it is rotating'
tíri 'he gives a start'	*tirírita* 'he is trembling'
wíwa 'he stumbles'	*wiwáwata* 'he is hobbling along'
kʷíla 'he takes a step forward'	*kʷilálata* 'he walks forward'
rípi 'it gives a flash'	*ripípita* 'it is sparkling'
ʔími 'it makes a bang'	*ʔimímita* 'it is thundering'
ngáro 'his teeth strike something hard'	*ngarórota* 'he is chewing on something hard'

You can see how this works, and it's clearly an elegant and economical system. Whorf's suggestion is, though, that, whereas English-speakers perceive 'taking a step' and 'walking' as rather different activities, Hopi speakers see them as aspects of a single activity, just as English-speakers do with *he walks* and *he walked*.

Another North American language, Navaho, has an extraordinarily rich vocabulary for talking about lines of various shapes, colours and configurations. Here is a small sample of the hundred or so different words available:

dzígai 'a white line running off into the distance'
adziisgai 'a group of parallel white lines running off into the
    distance'
hadziisgai 'a white line running vertically upward from the bottom
    to the top of an object'
ahééhesgai 'more than two white lines forming concentric circles'
áłch'inidzigai 'two white lines coming together at a point'
áłnánágah 'a white line zigzagging back and forth'

This large vocabulary allows Navaho speakers to speak effortlessly
about all kinds of geometrical arrangements which in English would
require lengthy descriptions. Again, though, the suggestion is that
Navaho speakers actually *perceive* the world differently from
English-speakers, that they perceive it in the geometrical terms
provided so naturally by their language. It is noteworthy that Navaho
place names are overwhelmingly geometrical in nature. For example,
a certain striking rock formation in Arizona is called in Navaho *Tsé
Áhé'ii'áhá*, literally, 'two rocks standing vertically parallel in a
reciprocal relationship to each other'. In English, the same rocks are
called 'Elephant's Feet'. English-speakers, it is suggested, see objects
as resembling other objects, while Navaho speakers see geometrical
relationships.

   Whorf found even more striking differences between North
American and European languages. One of his examples is the English
sentence *He invites people to a feast*, in which a complex notion is
broken up by English into such smaller elements of meaning as *invite*,
people and *feast*. In the Nootka language of British Columbia, the
equivalent sentence is a single word: *Tl'imshya'isita'itlma*. This
consists of the stem *tl'imsh-* 'boil' with five suffixes: *tl'imsh-ya-'is-ita-
'itl-ma*. The suffix *-ya* means '-ed', while the remaining suffixes mean
'eat', '-ers', 'go-for' and 'he-does'. A crude but literal English
rendering might be 'He does something involving going for eaters of
boiled [food]'. Nootka, Whorf argues, breaks up the same complex
activity in a different way from English: there is, he says, nothing
corresponding to 'invite' or 'people' or 'feast'; rather, the basic units of
meaning are things like 'cook', 'eat' and 'do something'.

   That different languages divide up the world differently is not in doubt. But the Sapir–Whorf view goes on to claim that speakers of these languages actually perceive the world differently, as a result of the different structures of their languages, and this conclusion is deeply controversial. In retrospect, it is clear that Whorf often exaggerated the differences between North American and European languages, but linguists are still arguing today about whether the hypothesis of linguistic relativity has any validity or not.

Undoubtedly the most famous test of the Sapir–Whorf hypothesis lies in the domain of colour terms, and here the results have been somewhat unexpected. Every language has a set of what we call **basic colour terms**. English, for example, is usually thought to have exactly eleven: *black*, *white*, *red*, *green*, *blue*, *yellow*, *orange*, *purple*, *grey*, *brown* and *pink* (some people have a different name for *purple*, but this doesn't matter). Other colour terms, such as *scarlet*, *lime green*, *red–orange* and *blonde*, are non-basic for one reason or another. Other languages have different numbers of basic colour terms: Nez Percé (North America) has seven, Ibo (Nigeria) has four, and Jalé (New Guinea) has just two. In each language, the whole range of colours is divided up among the available colour terms. So, for example, in Hanunóo (Philippines), the four colour terms work like this: (*ma*)*biru* covers black and the darker shades of brown, blue and purple; (*ma*)*lagti?* covers white and the paler shades of pink, blue and yellow; (*ma*)*rara?* covers red, orange and maroon; and (*ma*)*la-tuy* covers yellow and the lighter shades of green and brown.

Given the wide variation in systems of colour terminology, colour terms have often been regarded as a paradigm case of different languages dividing up the world differently, and hence perhaps also as a confirming instance of the Sapir–Whorf hypothesis. If an English-speaker insists that this pencil is yellow but that that one is green, while a Hanunóo speaker insists they're both (*ma*)*latuy*, does it follow that they are looking at the world differently?

Some decades ago, the anthropologists Brent Berlin and Paul Kay decided to look into this question. They tested the use of colour terms by people speaking dozens of different languages with different numbers of basic colour terms. First, they looked at the boundaries of colour terms. Clearly, the fewer terms a language has, the greater the territory which each must cover, and that's what Berlin and Kay found. They also found, of course, that the boundaries of colour terms are very fuzzy. English-speakers are typically very uncertain about just where red shades off into orange, pink or purple, and speakers of all languages show the same uncertainty with their own terms.

But then Berlin and Kay asked their subjects to choose, from a colour chart, the most central or typical example of each colour term. This time the results were not fuzzy at all: English-speakers all agree very closely as to just which shade of red constitutes the most central variety of red – it's roughly the shade that used to be called 'lipstick red' in the days when lipstick didn't come in 7,000 colours – and, interestingly, speakers of all languages show similar agreement about these central shades of all of their colour terms. Berlin and Kay call these central shades *foci*.

Now we come to the truly astonishing part of Berlin and Kay's findings. While languages have different numbers of colour terms with different extensions for each, *the foci are always the same*. More precisely, the locations of the foci appear to be genuinely universal, and each language seems to use a subset of the available foci. For example, the foci of the four Hanunóo terms *(ma)biru*, *(ma)lagti?*, *(ma)rara?* and *(ma)latuy* exactly match the foci of the English terms *black*, *white*, *red* and *green*, respectively. Hence the real difference between English and Hanunóo is that English has added a few more foci to the four of Hanunóo, but without changing those four.

Indeed, all the languages that Berlin and Kay studied showed the same pattern: a selection from a possible maximum of about eleven universal foci, with each language choosing two, three, four or more of these foci. Furthermore, the order in which these foci are chosen is also predictable. The first two chosen are always black and white, and the third one (if chosen) is red. The fourth is either green or yellow, and the fifth is the other one of these, while the sixth is always blue and the seventh is always brown. After seven, the remaining colour foci of pink, grey, purple and orange can be added in any order. Thus, a language with six colour terms (such as Plains Tamil of India) necessarily has black, white, red, green, yellow and blue, and not something else.

These are stunning findings. Colour terminology, formerly a happy hunting ground for linguistic relativists, has seemingly been shown to be governed by rigorous universal principles, and differences among languages are possible only within strict guidelines.

Berlin and Kay's pioneering work has spawned a large literature, and a few counterexamples have turned up here and there, but their conclusions still seem to be essentially valid. This is not the end of the story, however. The psychologists Lucy and Schweder have more recently demonstrated that the ability to remember colours is closely related to the colour terms of the language: the more basic colour terms a language has, the more accurately its speakers can remember colours. These findings suggest that Berlin and Kay's universal rules are not the whole story, and that some element of linguistic relativism must still be present. The validity or lack of it of the Sapir–Whorf hypothesis remains a subject of controversy.

Finally, before I leave this topic, I can't resist the chance to say something about another example discussed by Whorf: the Eskimos and their words for 'snow'. Very likely you've heard something about Eskimo words for 'snow'. If there is one thing that the average person knows about any language, it is that Eskimo has a whole bunch of words for 'snow'. But how many are there? Unfortunately, the various sources do not agree: some say fifty, some say a hundred, some say two hundred, and at least one claims four hundred. Who's right?

To begin with, there is no single Eskimo language. There are two major languages spoken by Eskimos, Inuit and Yupik, and each of these is spoken in several very divergent dialects. Hence the answer may be somewhat different, depending on which variety we're looking at, but it probably won't be wildly different. Still, we'd better choose one. Let's take West Greenlandic Inuit, since that variety has been intensively studied by linguists for generations, and since we have a comprehensive dictionary for it. How many different words for 'snow' can be found in that dictionary?

Two. Just two: *qanik* 'snow in the air' or 'snowflake' and *aput* 'snow on the ground'. That's it. That's all there is.

To be fair, the American anthropologist and linguist Franz Boas, commenting in passing on an unidentified variety of Inuit, claimed to have found a much larger number of words for 'snow': four. He reports, in his 1911 book, the words *aput* 'snow on the ground', *gana* 'falling snow', *piqsirpoq* 'drifting snow' and *qimuqsuq* 'snowdrift'.

Two or four, this is still a pretty far cry from four hunded, or even from fifty. In fact, it's not very different from English. English has at least *snow* (the most general term), *slush* ('wet snow on the ground'), *blizzard* ('quite a lot of snow falling at one time') and *sleet* (in its British sense of 'snow melting as it falls', and not in the North American sense of 'frozen rain'), but every skier will be able to add several further words for various types of snow: *powder*, *crust*, *hardpack*, and probably others. The likelihood is that any English-speaking skier has more words for different types of snow than any inhabitant of Alaska or Greenland.

Language and context

One of the most striking and important things about language is the way in which we use utterances to express meanings that aren't there. Consider the following exchange:

A: Where was John last night?
B: Well, there was a yellow Beetle parked outside Susie's place this morning.

On the face of it, this is an idiotic response to a simple question. The questioner has asked about John's whereabouts, but the responder has said not one word about John, and has instead brought up Susie and a Beetle, neither of which was being asked about. Nevertheless, you will agree, I'm sure, that the response is perfectly normal and reasonable. As long as the questioner knows that John drives a yellow Beetle (and perhaps even if she didn't know that before), the point of the response is obvious: the responder is saying, in effect, 'I don't *know* where John was last night, but I have reason to believe he spent the night with Susie'.

How on earth can things work like this? How can the questioner realize that such a seemingly irrelevant answer is actually intended to be informative, and how can she work out just what the point of the answer is supposed to be?

It's certainly not possible to maintain that the responder's utterance actually *means* 'John spent the night with Susie'. Look what happens if I change the question to something else:

> A: I hear John is giving Susie a really nice present for her birthday.
> B: Well, there was a yellow Beetle parked outside Susie's place this morning.

This time the questioner is probably going to interpret the response as meaning 'I think maybe John is giving Susie a Beetle for her birthday'. This is exactly the same response as before, but this time it gets a completely different interpretation. This is what I mean by saying that utterances can express meanings which are not really there – and, when you think about it, that's really rather stunning.

The key point here is the importance of the *context* in which an utterance is made. We don't say things in a vacuum, but rather we say them in a context which is partly linguistic (the things that have been said previously) and partly non-linguistic (the circumstances in which the speakers find themselves, including their knowledge of the world, their experience and their expectations). And we take advantage of *all* of this stuff when we interpret what other people are saying.

Given this fact, it might seem as though the enterprise of accounting for the meanings of utterances is going to be impossibly complex – and recall that it was just this overwhelming complexity that persuaded some linguists to give up on the whole business. And it certainly is complex. If you hold out an object and then let go of it, you know that it will fall to the floor; if it's a china cup, you know that it will probably shatter. The people who are working on artificial intelligence have to teach these things, very laboriously, to their computer programs, because otherwise the programs won't know anything about such concepts as gravity and fragility.

Nevertheless, in spite of the daunting nature of the task, linguists have been able to make some useful progress in explaining how we communicate meanings. The first key step was an appreciation that there are at least two different ways of extracting meaning from an utterance. One way is just to note the content of the utterance itself, the words it contains and their grammatical arrangement. This kind of meaning is intrinsic to the utterance, and it will always be there, no matter what the context. Accounting for this more straight-forward type of meaning is the business of semantics, as we now understand the term. The other way of extracting meaning is by comparing the utterance with the context, in the way I have just been illustrating. Here the meaning is derived, not from the utterance alone, but from the combination of the utterance and its context. And to the study of how such meanings are obtained we give a new name: **pragmatics**. Pragmatics is the study of meaning which is derived from context, and we now recognize that it is different from semantics and requires different approaches.

One of the most influential approaches to pragmatics is that proposed by the philosopher of language Paul Grice. Grice formu-lated a number of rules governing the way in which utterances are understood in context; these rules are called **Grice's maxims**. Two of these maxims are the Maxim of Relevance, which simply says 'Make your contribution relevant', and the Maxim of Quantity, which says 'Say as much as you are in a position to say.' Consider now how these maxims apply to my first Beetle example.

The questioner asks where John was last night, and is told only that there was a yellow Beetle outside Susie's place this morning. Assuming that the responder is obeying the maxims, the questioner reasons more or less as follows: 'The reply must be relevant, so it must be intended as an answer to my question. By Quantity, the responder doesn't know where John was, or he would simply have told me. But he's mentioned a yellow Beetle, and I know John drives a yellow Beetle, so, by Relevance, I am meant to understand that this is very probably John's car he's bringing up. Since I'm told that car was outside Susie's place this morning, it follows that John was probably there, too. Since I couldn't find him last night, the best guess is that John was at Susie's last night, and therefore that he spent the night there.'

Of course, we don't consciously work through such an elaborate chain of reasoning, but that is none the less a slowed-down version of what must be going on in our heads when we converse. And we are very good at this sort of reasoning. We do it so quickly and effortlessly that most of the time we're not even aware of what we're doing, and it appears that we do it by taking advantage of principles of conversation like Grice's maxims.

Of course, it would be too much to claim that every speaker always cooperates fully all of the time – that nobody is ever evasive, dishonest or unhelpful. But one of the most fascinating things to come out of Grice's work is the realization that, rather frequently, people deliberately violate the maxims at a superficial level in order to be cooperative at a deeper level. This behaviour is called **flouting** the maxims. Here is a genuine example that I encountered once.

Years ago, when I was a lowly postgraduate student, I happened to be in my supervisor's office one day when the phone rang. I could only hear one end of the conversation, but it was clear what was going on. Another student – let's call him Herbie – was just finishing his PhD and was applying for jobs, and the caller was asking my boss for a reference on Herbie. Here is what I heard:

> 'Oh, he's a very pleasant fellow – everyone likes him.'
> [*pause*]
> 'Well, he's very good-natured – I'm sure he'd get on well with everyone at your place.'
> [*pause*]
> 'Yes, he's certainly very pleasant, and I believe he's quite popular.'

At that point the caller gave up. Now: do you think Herbie got the job? I am quite certain he did not. But why not? After all, my boss was saying nothing but nice things about him.

But, of course, they weren't the *right* nice things. The caller was interested in Herbie's capacity for research, and he was hoping to hear something like 'Herbie is an outstanding researcher, and he'll do first-class work for you.' Instead, he got nothing but remarks about Herbie's agreeable personality. In spite of persistent questioning by the caller, my boss resolutely refused to say one word about Herbie's work. On the face of it, then, he was grossly violating the maxims of both Relevance and Quantity. At a deeper level, however, he was still cooperating, because the caller could reason as follows: 'If he had anything good to say about Herbie's work, he would say it. But he says nothing, which can only mean that he has nothing good to say.

Therefore I can safely conclude that Herbie is not a good researcher, which is what I wanted to know.'

We all do this sort of thing all the time, and knowing how to communicate successfully in such indirect ways is one of the things we have to master in order to be fully fluent users of English. Grice's maxims seem to provide a good description of the way English-speakers behave, but do the same rules also work for other languages?

There is clear evidence that other languages may have different rules. In Australian languages, for example, a high degree of explicitness is considered socially desirable, while avoidable vagueness is held to be a fault. Consequently, an Australian speaker using the everyday style will never use a generic term like 'tree' or 'lizard' if he can possibly use a more specific term for the particular sort of tree or lizard, and he will never use a vague word like 'go' if he can say instead 'go uphill on foot': Australian languages are accordingly rich in such specific words. We might guess, then, that my former supervisor's behaviour would not be considered reasonable or acceptable by native Australians. (Incidentally, it was precisely this reluctance to use generic terms that misled early European investigators into concluding (wrongly) that Australian languages didn't have any generics, and even (grotesquely wrongly) that Australians were incapable of formulating generalizations. This is a signal reminder of how deeply ingrained our rules of conversation are.)

On the other hand, speakers of Malagasy, the chief language of Madagascar, are exceedingly reluctant to be explicit about anything, and Malagasy speech is characterized by a very high degree of non-committal vagueness. Elinor Ochs Keenan, the linguist who has studied Malagasy most carefully, advances two reasons for this behaviour. First, Malagasy is mainly spoken in small, closed villages where new information is rare and is accordingly highly prized; knowing something that others don't know confers prestige, and speakers are unwilling to part with such prestige. Second, in Malagasy society it is considered deeply shameful to say anything which might possibly bring embarrassment to anyone else, or even to make a prediction which turns out to be inaccurate, and speakers therefore go to great lengths to avoid these outcomes by saying as

71

little as possible. Westerners in Madagascar are, as a consequence, constantly bewildered by their inability to get straight answers to even simple questions. It seems clear that Grice's Maxim of Quantity does not hold in Malagasy, and that Malagasy speech is governed by somewhat different rules from our own.

Further reading

The best elementary introduction to semantics is Hurford and Heasley (1983). Somewhat more demanding textbooks include Leech (1974), Hoffman (1993) and Frawley (1992); the last two both contain chapters on tense. Tense systems in general are described in Comrie (1985). Word meaning is covered in Jackson (1988), which is largely orientated toward dictionary writing, and Cruse (1986). Useful introductions to pragmatics are Levinson (1983) and Mey (1993). Whorf's work is collected in Whorf (1956), and a very readable book on the cross-cultural aspects of language is Bonvillain (1993). Berlin and Kay's work on colour terms is presented in Berlin and Kay (1969). Australian avoidance styles are described in Dixon (1980), and Dyirbal in particular in Dixon (1972). The discussion of Eskimo words for 'snow' is taken from the title essay in Pullum (1991), a wonderful collection of essays which includes discussions of such topics as linguistic fascism and the way visiting linguists are viewed by hotel managers, as well as an interview with Noam Chomsky conducted by *Star Trek*'s Mr Spock.

Chapter 4

Variation in language

Like many other people, I have so far been using the language name *English* as though there were not the slightest doubt about just what this name referred to. And of course it's true that we rarely have any trouble in distinguishing English from, say, French or Chinese. But that label 'English' is in fact a good deal slipperier than you might have supposed. Let's see why.

graphical variation

Are you confident that you can recognize English when you see it? Consider the following examples, and see what you think about them:

(4.1) We had us a real nice house.
(4.2) She's a dinky-di Pommie sheila.
(4.3) I might could do it.
(4.4) The lass divn't gan to the pictures, pet.
(4.5) They're a lousy team any more.
(4.6) I am not knowing where to find a stepney.

73

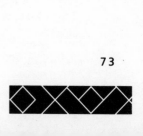

What's your reaction to each of these? Is it normal? Is it familiar? Is it understandable? Is it English?

The answers you give will depend partly on your personal experience but perhaps more importantly on where you come from. Each of these utterances is in fact perfectly normal and unremarkable in some part of the English-speaking world, but is not normal at all elsewhere. Since it's unlikely that you've spent time in every English-speaking corner of the planet, some of my examples will doubtless seem very strange to you, and one or two may actually be incomprehensible.

Yet the people who use these forms regard themselves as speakers of English and are regarded as speakers of English by other speakers of English. A speaker from the appropriate geographical area would produce one of these utterances without thinking about it, and would very likely be surprised to learn that other speakers find the utterance strange or difficult.

What we are looking at here is one type of **variation** in language – specifically, geographical variation. Like most other languages, English is spoken differently in different places: that is, it exhibits **regional dialects**. You will certainly be aware already of the existence of regional dialects, and you will probably be able to recognize some of them when you hear them, even if you're occasionally surprised or puzzled by what you hear. (You may also have a strong emotional reaction to some of them, but that is a topic we will consider in Chapter 8.)

And my examples? Well, (4.1), with its extra *us*, is typical of much of the south of the USA, and is occasionally heard elsewhere. Example (4.2) is, of course, Australian, and it means 'She's a typical Englishwoman'. Example (4.3), which means 'I might be able to do it', is quite normal in many parts of Scotland and also in parts of the Appalachian Mountain region of the USA. Example (4.4) you may recognize as 'Geordie' – that is, as the speech of the Tyneside area of northeastern England; it means 'The girl didn't go to the cinema'. Example (4.5), which many British speakers find mysterious, is typical of a large part of the northeastern USA; it means, roughly, 'They used to be a good team but now they're lousy' – in other words, it means exactly the opposite of *They're not a lousy team any more*.

Finally, (4.6) is an example of the English spoken in India, and it means 'I don't know where to find a spare wheel'.

These examples briefly illustrate some of the wide variation in grammar and vocabulary which can be found across the English-speaking world. Even more familiarly, perhaps, variation also affects pronunciation. You will certainly have noticed that other speakers of English often pronounce the language differently from the way you do. That is, different speakers have different **accents**. An accent is simply a particular way of pronouncing a language, and it is important to realize that *every* speaker has an accent. It is not just the Glasgow bricklayer, the New York taxi driver, or the Jamaican pop singer who has an accent: I have an accent, you have an accent, the Queen of England has an accent. Every speaker necessarily speaks the language with some accent or other. Of course, you will certainly regard some accents as more familiar, or as more prestigious, than others, but this cannot change the fact that every speaker has an accent.

The purely phonetic differences among accents are great enough that you can easily distinguish the accents of England, Scotland, Australia, North America and the Caribbean, and perhaps you can quickly spot a speaker who comes from Liverpool, Glasgow or New York. But recall that I pointed out in Chapter 1 that not all speakers of English have the same set of phonemes – that is, we don't all have the same set of consonants and vowels. And, even when we do, we don't all use them in the same places. As a result of these facts, there are many pairs of English words which are pronounced identically by some English-speakers but differently by others.

Here are a few examples of such pairs. Try saying each pair to yourself, and decide whether you pronounce the two words identically or differently. Each pair is followed by some brief comments about who uses which type of pronunciation, but note that my comments are unavoidably very rough and broad, and that you won't necessarily have the type of pronunciation described as typical of your region.

1   **farther** and **father**: These are pronounced identically by most people in England (except in the southwest and parts of the

north) and in Wales, by almost everyone in Australia, New Zealand and South Africa, and by many people in the south and on the east coast of the USA. Other speakers distinguish them.

2　**whine** and **wine**: These are distinguished by most Scottish and Irish speakers, by many Americans and Canadians, and by some New Zealanders. Almost everyone else pronounces them identically, and this type of pronunciation is gaining ground in the USA.　．

3　**cot** and **caught**: These are pronounced identically by almost all Canadians, by many Scots and by some Americans; everyone else distinguishes them. (By the way, this is often a useful way of distinguishing Canadians from Americans, but it won't be for long: the difference seems to be rapidly disappearing in the States.)

4　**horse** and **hoarse**: These are distinguished by most people in Scotland and Ireland and by some Americans; almost everyone else pronounces them identically.

5　**stir** and **stare**: These are identical for most speakers from the Liverpool area and for many speakers in Manchester (England); they are different for everyone else.

6　**poor** and **pour**: These are different for most Scots and for many North Americans; most others pronounce them identically.

7　**threw** and **through**: These are different for most speakers in Wales and for a few people in England and in the USA; almost everyone else pronounces them identically.

8　**dew** and **do**: These are identical for most North Americans and for some speakers in East Anglia; most others distinguish them, though there are signs that the difference is beginning to disappear in other parts of England.

Very many other pairs of words could be adduced to make the same point: **pore** and **paw**; **pull** and **pool**; **marry** and **merry** (and also **Mary**); **buck** and **book**; **toe** and **tow**; **hair** and **air**; **three** and **free**; **higher** and **hire**; and many, many others. You may find it surprising that other English-speakers make a distinction you don't make, or fail to make one you do make; you may even find one or two of my examples hard to believe. But there is absolutely no doubt of the facts: for every one of these pairs, the two words are pronounced identically by some speakers and differently by others. Variation in the pronunciation of English is far greater than we might have expected from our personal experience.

By the way, this impressive variation constitutes a severe obstacle to any attempts at reforming the admittedly erratic spelling system of English. It's all very well to suggest that we should spell our words the way we pronounce them, but whose pronunciation should serve as the basis of a simplified spelling? Should *threw* and *through*, or *whine* and *wine*, or *horse* and *hoarse*, be spelled identically or differently in a reformed spelling? Not infrequently, a would-be spelling reformer has simply assumed that '*my* pronunciation' should be the basis of a simplified spelling, but, as you can see, this is hardly a constructive approach. One of the few advantages of our bizarre spelling system is that it serves all English-speakers equally well by serving us all equally badly.

English is in no way unusual in its regional variation. Every language which is spoken over a significant stretch of territory shows comparable variation: Spanish, French, Italian, Arabic, Chinese, and so on. Even Basque, spoken only in a region about 100 miles by 30 miles, exhibits prodigious regional variation, perhaps greater than anything found in English. Indeed, English is, if anything, rather remarkable in the degree of regional uniformity which it presents, particularly across the vast North American and Australian continents.

Other types of variation

Regional dialects and accents are perhaps the most conspicuous type of variation in language, but they are far from being the only type. Substantial variation can be found in a single community, and even in the speech of a single individual. Here are some further examples of English to consider, all of them this time taken from the English of the London area in southeast England. What can you say about the likely context of each of these?

77

(4.7)   Would you mind very much if I were to open a window?

(4.8)   Ta, mate.

(4.9)   Oh, Julia, what an absolutely divine tunic!

(4.10) All monies owing in respect of 2(d) above shall be payable not later than the date of completion specified therein.

(4.11) I refer the Right Honourable gentleman to my previous answer.

(4.12) Yanks 2, Planks 0.

Here, (4.7) was surely uttered by a middle-class speaker in a somewhat formal context – not relaxing among friends – while (4.8) was undoubtedly uttered by a working-class speaker, since *ta* 'thanks' and *mate* 'sir' are conspicuous markers of working-class London speech. Example (4.9), as you will have guessed, was spoken by a woman: the words *divine* and *tunic* are rarely used by men, and admiring one another's clothes is far more acceptable for women than for men. Rather different is (4.10), whose stiff, impersonal style and use of such unusual words as *monies* and *therein* reveals it as taken from a legal document. The formulaic nature of (4.11) places it immediately into the House of Commons and probably into Question Time. Finally, (4.12) could only be a headline in a popular tabloid newspaper: its typically brief and brash style simultaneously reports the result of a soccer match between England and the USA and comments bluntly on the English team's performance.

These examples illustrate some of the considerable variation which can be found in a single community. First, different types of people speak differently: middle-class speakers don't talk like working-class speakers; women speak differently from men; older people speak differently from younger people. Second, the same person speaks differently in different contexts: our middle-class speaker in (4.7) would surely have said something different in a more relaxed environment, and the minister in (4.11) would probably not use this particular phrasing outside of Question Time, except as a joke. Finally, the medium of expression matters: though legal documents admittedly represent something of an extreme, most types of written English are noticeably different from spoken English.

If you have some experience of London, then all of my

examples will be more or less familiar to you; if you don't, then you will none the less be familiar with comparable examples of variation in your own region. A speaker learning a first language in childhood simultaneously acquires a substantial amount of control over this variation. A middle-class speaker learns to say *Thank you very much* and to avoid *Ta, mate*; a man learns not to make enthusiastic remarks about clothes; every educated speaker acquires some degree of control over formal written varieties of English. Further, everyone learns to recognize the significance of variants which she or he does not personally use: when you encounter someone else's English, you can almost always draw some important conclusions about what kind of person you are dealing with. Finally, every speaker learns to control some range of variation: you can effortlessly switch between the sort of English appropriate when you're chatting to close friends in a pub or a bar and the kind of English appropriate when you're being interviewed for a job. Any speaker of English who tried to use the same style of speech in such disparate circumstances would be regarded as very odd indeed.

Studying variation

The study of variation has something of a chequered history in linguistics. Regional dialects attracted attention quite early, and more than a century ago European linguists were already pursuing the discipline we call **dialectology**: the study of regional dialects. The dialectologists have accumulated vast quantities of data from regional varieties of English, French, German and other languages, and they have often presented their findings in the convenient form of maps. Figure 4.1 is a simplified dialect map of England showing the usual local word for 'young female person' in the early years of this century; the lines separating different regional forms are called **isoglosses**. A similar map constructed today would show a very different result, since the southeastern (and standard English) word *girl* has all but wiped out its competitors, except for *lass*, which survives in the north.

Figure 4.2 is a rather more detailed dialect map showing the local words for 'dragonfly' in the eastern USA; it shows that the

FIGURE 4.1 Words for 'girl' in England
Source: Reprinted with permission from P. Trudgill (1990), *The Dialects of England*, Oxford: Blackwell, p. 116.

isoglosses between forms are rarely as neat as the first map would suggest.

As a result of the efforts of the dialect geographers, we know a great deal about regional variation in English and other languages. Other types of variation, however, did not attract early attention. For

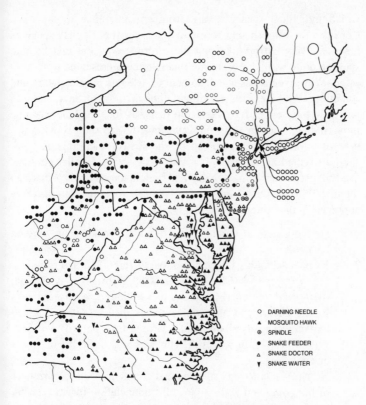

FIGURE 4.2 Words for 'dragonfly' in the eastern USA
Source: Reprinted with permission from H. Kurath (1949) *Word Geography of the Eastern United States,* Ann Arbor: University of Michigan Press.

most of this century, variation within communities was largely ignored. At best, such variation was regarded as too unsystematic to be amenable to study; at worst, it was dismissed as peripheral, insignificant, even a nuisance. In the 1960s, however, linguists pursuing **sociolinguistics** – the study of the relation between language and society – began to turn their attention to such variation, and within a few years they had begun to report some extraordinary findings.

Some of their most striking findings concerned the way in

which individual speakers vary from one utterance to the next. Consider the English *-ing* forms like *going*. Most English-speakers have two ways of pronouncing these forms: one that matches the spelling quite well, and a second that is often represented in writing as *goin'*. A given speaker will sometimes use one pronunciation and sometimes the other, in a seemingly unpredictable manner, and it is precisely this sort of **free variation** that was long considered to be impossible to study in a fruitful way. Nevertheless, the *going ~ goin'* type of variation was examined by the British sociolinguist Peter Trudgill in the English city of Norwich in the 1970s. For this purpose, Trudgill used a new approach that had been invented by the American linguist William Labov only a few years before: the **quantitative** approach. What Trudgill did was this:

1   He collected a number of Norwich speakers of varying backgrounds.

2   He put each of his subjects into four different types of situation: (a) *casual speech* (CS), that is, relaxed, informal conversation; (b) *formal speech* (FS), the self-conscious speech used in a formal interview; (c) *reading-passage speech* (RPS), in which the subject reads aloud from a written text; and (d) *word-list speech* (WLS), in which the subject reads out a list of words one at a time.

3   He tape-recorded his subjects and counted all the occurrences of the *going* and *goin'* styles of pronunciation for all relevant words.

4   Using independent criteria, he assigned each of his subjects to one of five social classes: the *lower working class* (LWC), the *middle working class* (MWC), the *upper working class* (UWC), the *lower middle class* (LMC) and the *middle middle class* (MMC).

5   Finally, for each of his five classes, he calculated the *average* number of *goin'*-style pronunciations in *each* of the four situations and converted this figure to a percentage of all relevant items.

This final percentage Trudgill called the *(ng) index*: the higher this index, the more frequently speakers are using the *goin'* type of

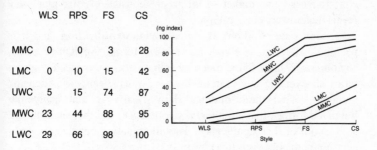

	WLS	RPS	FS	CS
MMC	0	0	3	28
LMC	0	10	15	42
UWC	5	15	74	87
MWC	23	44	88	95
LWC	29	66	98	100

FIGURE 4.3 Percentages of *-in'* forms in Norwich
Source: Adapted from P. Trudgill (1974) *The Social Differentiation of English in Norwich*, Cambridge: Cambridge University Press.

pronunciation and the less frequently they are using the *going* style. Trudgill's results are shown in Figure 4.3, both as a numerical table and as a graph.

Observe the striking patterns which emerge from Trudgill's work. Every group of speakers, and indeed every individual speaker, uses both types of pronunciation in most or all situations. But, on the one hand, every speaker uses a steadily greater proportion of *-in'* forms as the context becomes more informal, as shown by the rising graph for each group. And, on the other hand, in any given situation, a member of a lower-ranking social group uses a higher proportion of *-in'* forms than a member of a higher-ranking group, as shown by the fact that the lines on the graph never cross.

These patterns only become apparent when the variation is examined from a quantitative – that is, a statistical – point of view: it is generally impossible to predict which form any speaker will use on any particular occasion. Statistically speaking, though, the behaviour of individual speakers is remarkably consistent. Furthermore, if we didn't already know it, we could determine by examining the graph that *-ing* pronunciations are regarded as socially more presti- gious than *-in'* pronunciations: every speaker shifts toward *-ing* forms as the context becomes more formal, leading to greater self-

83

consciousness, and higher social groups consistently use more -*ing* forms than lower social groups.

This state of affairs is called **social stratification**, and it is peculiar neither to Norwich nor to -*ing* forms. Again and again, sociolinguists have found much the same pattern in speech communities all over the world, involving a very wide range of linguistic variables. What these findings show clearly is that competing linguistic forms often have *social significance*, and that speakers are well aware of that significance. This illuminating conclusion, however, immediately leads to a new puzzle.

Language and identity

If it's true that speakers are aware of the social significance of competing forms, that they can often produce the prestige forms, and that, in certain contexts, they can shift strongly toward the use of prestige forms, then there is an obvious question: why don't most or all speakers simply abandon low-prestige forms altogether and switch to high-prestige forms? Why should anyone persist in using forms which he or she recognizes as being of low prestige? The question gains added force when we realize that working-class speakers regularly characterize their own speech as 'not very good English' and not infrequently profess to admire middle-class speech.

The easiest way of answering this question is to consider a hypothetical example. Imagine a plumber or a motor mechanic in London who speaks the typical working-class English of his area. And suppose that he, dissatisfied with his own speech and impressed by the middle-class English of television newsreaders or of his well-paid customers, decided to try to abandon his ordinary speech in favour of the best approximation to middle-class English he could muster. What would be the result? Would his friends and family be favourably impressed? Would they admire his prestige speech and even try to copy him?

Certainly not. Instead, they would find his efforts comical for about ten seconds, and then they would become increasingly annoyed, distant and perhaps even hostile. Very soon our ambitious plumber or mechanic would find himself with no friends left. But why? After all, everybody enjoys prestige, and prestige is prestige, isn't it?

No, it isn't. In talking glibly about 'prestige forms', I have overlooked something vitally important – something that's related to one of the central functions of language.

One of the functions of language? Isn't the function of language just communication? Again, the answer is 'no'. Every person needs to maintain an individual identity. One of the most important aspects of that identity is membership of a group, and language provides a powerful way of maintaining and demonstrating group membership. Our plumber will belong to a group of family and friends with whom he has shared experiences, shared interests, shared circumstances and shared values. In order to remain a member of that group, he must speak like the other members of the group. For this purpose, it doesn't matter whether the group's speech is independently regarded, by him or by anybody else, as of high or low prestige. What's important is to speak the way the others do, because doing so carries the clear message 'I regard myself as a member of your group.'

But when our plumber deliberately tries to change his speech to something quite different, he is announcing in the clearest possible terms 'I no longer regard myself as a member of your group'. If he persists, the others will quickly get the message, and he will soon find himself excluded from their group. Language is a very powerful means of declaring and maintaining one's identity, and there is no reason to suppose that this function is less important to most people than communicating information. Linguists sometimes apply the term **covert prestige** to the status of linguistic forms which are of low prestige in the community as a whole but which are of crucial importance in maintaining a speaker's position in a particular social group.

Of course, sometimes a speaker really does undertake a change in speech. Not a few of my academic colleagues grew up speaking a regional or social variety of English with low prestige, and spent years acquiring the sort of middle-class English considered appropriate in university circles – indeed, I myself, with my solidly working-class background, am one such. But all of us, of course, have been broadcasting the same message as my hypothetical plumber: we no longer consider ourselves part of the social circle we grew up in, and instead we want it to be known that we consider ourselves part of a very different group – the group of professional academics.

Language, sex and gender

Perhaps one of the most obvious social divisions in society is that between men and women, and this division, not surprisingly, is often strongly represented in speech. In some languages, the difference is so great that men and women actually use different words, different pronunciations or different grammatical forms. This happens, for example, in Japanese, in which some words are different:

Women's form	Men's form	Meaning
onaka	*hara*	'stomach'
taberu	*kuu*	'eat'
atashi	*boku*	'I'
ohiya	*mizu*	'water'
oishii	*umai*	'delicious'

Similarly, in Koasati, a language spoken in Louisiana, many words have different endings when used by women and by men. For example, the word meaning 'lift it' is *lakawhol* in women's speech but *lakawhos* in men's speech.

English has nothing quite on this scale, but investigation has shown that men and women do indeed speak rather differently in English, quite apart from the obvious fact that they tend to talk about different things: women spend more time talking about clothes and children, while men talk more about cars and sports. Here are a few of the differences which have sometimes been reported; be warned, however, that some of these reported differences are controversial.

1   Women are said to make frequent use of a number of admiring terms rarely used by men: *divine*, *cute*, *adorable*, *thrilling*, and others.
2   Women are said to make finer discriminations than men in certain areas, such as colour terms – that is, women are much

more likely to use precise terms such as *burgundy*, *ecru*, *chartreuse*, *crimson* and *beige*.

3   Men are said to swear much more than women. Well, this may have been true a generation ago, but, if the language of my female students is anything to go by, it's not true any more, though a few of the coarser expressions are perhaps still mainly used by men. (What do you suppose you'd say if you dropped a jar of mayonnaise, leaving a disgusting puddle of oily goo and glass shards on the floor?)

4   Women are said to use more *tag questions* than men – that is, they're more likely to say things like *It's nice, isn't it?*, as if to seek confirmation. (This claim is particularly controversial.)

5   Men interrupt far more than women. This usually comes as a surprise to men, who are convinced it's the other way round, but extensive research has demonstrated the truth of my statement beyond any possible doubt.

6   Women use more baby-talk than men.

7   Very generally, women's discourse is *cooperative*, while men's is *competitive*. That is, women in conversation usually seek to sympathize with one another and to support and admire the ideas and contributions of others. Men, in contrast, tend to try to outdo one another, to score points and to top what the others have said.

8   Finally, women are more likely than men of the same social group to use (overt) prestige forms, and are likely to report themselves as using more prestige forms than they actually do. Men do just the opposite: they use fewer prestige forms, and they report themselves as using even fewer than they do use.

Feminists have often pointed to these differences as evidence of the subordinate position of women in our society: women are expected to be 'ladylike', to defer to the pronouncements of men, to seek approval from men before asserting anything of substance, and to confine their discussions to topics considered trivial by men. Undoubtedly, the feminists are right in their interpretation. Some feminists, however, have gone further, and vigorously attacked what they see as the built-in sexism of English (and other languages). What do they mean by that?

You may be aware that, outside of term time, universities often hire out their facilities to conference meetings, in order to make some extra money. Some years ago, at the university at which I was then working, the conference authorities noticed that a sailors' conference had been booked in during the same week as a nurses' conference. Seeing an opportunity for boosting the bar takings, they therefore laid on a disco. Well, all the sailors and nurses turned up, all right, but the disco was rather less than an unqualified success. All the sailors were big, burly men, and all the nurses were – big, burly men. Rarely has there been a more desperate disc jockey.

It had not occurred to the organizers that nurses could be other than marriageable young women, or at least women. The word *nurse* is one of a number of profession names which are strongly sex-marked. Sailors, doctors, taxi drivers, judges – all are routinely expected to be men. But nurses, models, au pairs and secretaries (and also prostitutes!) are equally expected to be women. Not so long ago, these expectations were in fact very reliable, but times have changed, and today there are few jobs performed only by one sex. Well, we'll get used to novelties like male nurses, but the real problem, in the eyes of the critics, is the existence of explicitly sex-marked terms like *chairman*, *postman*, *fireman* on the one hand and *cleaning lady* and *tea lady* on the other. Dissatisfaction with these now often grossly unsuitable labels has led to the now widespread preference for alternative terms like *cleaner* or newly coined forms like *firefighter*. And every university department in the country now has a *chair*, rather than a *chairman* (or *chairwoman*).

Some terms, though, are harder to replace: at present, there appears to be no widely-used alternative to *postman*. (*Postperson*? *Postie*? *Postal deliveryperson*?) Worse still are the cases like *manhole*, *man-eating* (*shark*) and *to man* (*a position*). And worst of all is the generic use of unmodified *man* to mean 'human being', as in *Men first reached the Americas 13,000 years ago*. Women have been obliged to tolerate such usages for centuries, but now, it seems, we are slowly purging the language of such sexist usages.

How far should we go in this enterprise? You will have noticed that I have several times used such awkward locutions as *his or her*, as in *Why should anyone persist in using forms which he or she recognizes as being of low prestige?* The choice between sexist *he* and clumsy *he or she* in these cases is not an appealing one, but what can we do about it? Some people have gone so far as to propose a new pronoun, unmarked for sex, such as *herm* (a blend of *her* and *him*) or *han* (borrowed from Finnish, for heaven's sake), but few people can muster any enthusiasm for such drastic and possibly grotesque innovations. At present, no solution is in sight.

Life with two languages

Something of an extreme in language variation is represented by communities and individuals who use two (or more) different languages every day. English-speakers are notoriously bad at learning other languages, but a large proportion of the earth's population regularly use more than one language every day. In New Guinea, or in the Amazon rain forest, where many different languages are often spoken in quite small areas, people routinely learn the languages of two or three neighbouring groups as well as their own, and the same was true of Australia before the European settlement virtually destroyed the indigenous culture. Even in Europe, with its large, centralized, well-established nation–states, there are millions of people using more than one language.

Outsiders are not always aware of this. We typically expect people in France, for example, to speak French, and of course most adults in France do speak French. But several million French people in fact speak Dutch, Breton, Basque, Occitan ('Provençal'), Catalan, Corsican or Alsatian German as their first language, and not French. Wales has been part of Britain for nearly a thousand years, yet over half a million people in northern and western Wales speak Welsh as their first language, often beginning to learn English only after starting school. They speak Welsh at home, with their Welsh-speaking family and friends, but speak English with outsiders.

Centuries ago, all of Wales was Welsh-speaking, but the language has been steadily losing ground to the remorseless influence of English, the principal language of the United Kingdom. This influence has been exercised in various ways. On the one hand, Welsh-speakers have long realized that a knowledge of English would confer opportunities far beyond the borders of Wales. On the other, the British authorities have frequently persecuted the Welsh language: not so many years ago, for example, schoolchildren were punished for speaking Welsh in school. Understandably, many Welsh-speakers are deeply resentful of what they see as the gradual obliteration of their language and their culture by the spread of English, and some have reacted vigorously by means ranging from a refusal to speak English at all to arson attacks on houses owned by English-speakers. In some measure, of course, this is an economic issue: prosperous Londoners snap up cottages in picturesque north Wales as holiday homes, thereby driving the price of housing up to the point where the local people can no longer afford it. Primarily, though, the issue here is one of identity. We have already seen that an individual's speech is a powerful indicator of personal identity, and Wales is no exception. Many Welsh feel that they are in great danger of losing their identity as Welsh men and women, and of being reduced merely to anonymous if slightly quaint speakers of English on the margins of the English-speaking world.

Welsh is what we call a **minority language**. The term is slightly odd, since Welsh-speakers are in fact a majority in much of Wales, but they are a minority in Britain as a whole. Like some other European countries, Britain has recently been pursuing a somewhat more enlightened policy toward its minority languages. Welsh is no longer openly persecuted, and Welsh-language education, broadcasting and publication are now positively encouraged. Official forms and documents are now usually bilingual, and even legal proceedings can be conducted in Welsh. It remains to be seen, however, whether these steps will be adequate to save Welsh from the continuing pressure of its powerful neighbour, the world's most prestigious language, English.

Strangely enough, in the world's largest English-speaking country, the USA, it is the speakers of the dominant language, English, who have recently become fearful for the future of their language. In the USA, the hundreds of indigenous languages have mostly been extinguished or reduced to insignificance by the spread of English. Throughout American history, however, immigrants have been pouring into the USA from all over the world. At various times, huge numbers of speakers of German, Italian, Hungarian, Russian, Chinese, Vietnamese, and a hundred other languages, have settled in America. These **immigrant languages** have sometimes survived for several generations in particular communities. More often, however, the children of the immigrants have rapidly switched to English, in the process known to Americans as the 'melting pot'. But in the last couple of decades the influx of Spanish-speaking immigrants has reached floodlike proportions. Millions of Spanish-speakers have poured into the USA from Mexico, from Puerto Rico, from Cuba, from all over Latin America. Today, sizeable chunks of New York, Florida and the American southwest are predominantly Spanish-speaking, and Spanish is often the first language in such varied spheres as schooling, hospitals and local politics.

Faced with such a dramatic rise in the influence of Spanish, many English-speaking Americans have reacted defensively. Several states have passed laws declaring English to be their official language, and there is growing pressure on Washington to do the same for the whole country. (The USA, curiously perhaps, has no official language: it had never previously occurred to anyone to doubt the *de facto* position of English.)

Is there any real need for such laws? Personally, I doubt it. First, the position of English, not just in the USA but in the world, seems unassailable for the foreseeable future: English is everywhere the language of business, of technology, of communications, of science, and of popular culture. Second, if I'm wrong, and Spanish *is* destined to supplant English in the USA, I can't see that passing laws against it will have any effect: we might as well pass laws against inflation, or against dying of infectious diseases. Finally, so what if English does succumb to Spanish? Spanish is a rich and expressive language, and, like Latin and French before it, English cannot hope to be the world's premier language forever.

Further reading

There is a wealth of introductory reading on the topics touched on in this chapter. Among the best general introductions to sociolinguistics are Romaine (1994), Holmes (1992), Hudson (1980) and Trudgill

(1974). Hughes and Trudgill (1979) and Trudgill (1990) are readable introductions to the dialects of British English, while Milroy and Milroy (1993) surveys regional differences in English grammar throughout the British Isles. Trudgill and Chambers (1991) is a fascinating collection of short studies of regional varieties of English all over the world, and Trudgill and Hannah (1994) looks at variation in standard English in all the major English-speaking countries. Platt *et al* (1984) examines the use of English in countries where it is a major second language. Wells (1982) is a very comprehensive survey of all major accents of English, easy to read if you know a little phonetics. The most convenient introductions to dialectology in general are Trudgill (1994), which is very elementary, Chambers and Trudgill (1980) and Francis (1983). Among the huge number of works on men's and women's language, I might particularly recommend Coates (1993), Graddol and Swann (1989), Kramarae (1981), Miller and Swift (1980) and Spender (1985). And beyond a doubt the most stunning exhibition of the built-in sexism of English is Hofstadter (1985).

Chapter 5

Change in language

Consider the following passage:

> And hēo cende hire frum-cennedan sunu, and
> hine mid cild-clāþum bewand, and hine on
> binne ālegde for þǣm þe hīe næfdon rūm on
> cumena hūs. And hierdas wæron on þǣm ilcan
> rīce waciende, and niht-wæccan healdende ofer
> heora heorda. Þā stōd Dryhtnes engel wiþ hīe
> and Godes beorhtnes him ymbscān: and hīe him
> micelum ege adrēdon.

Can you make any sense of this? Probably not much,
unless you've had specialist training in this language.
You might be intrigued by the repeated appearance of
the word *and*, but otherwise the passage looks pretty
opaque.

Any guesses as to what language this is? Dutch?
Swedish? Icelandic? Something even more exotic?

Well, in fact, it's none of these. This passage is
written in English. Not the sort of English that you and
I use now, of course, but English none the less.

The passage was written nearly a thousand years ago by an English-speaker in the southwest of England, and it is written in the sort of English that people were speaking then. We call it **Old English**, or sometimes **Anglo-Saxon**. And to us this English is very strange indeed. You might be able to pick out the odd recognizable word here or there, but mostly this sort of English is as strange and unfamiliar to us as, say, modern Dutch.

But this isn't Dutch: it's English. The people who spoke this language taught it to their children, who taught it to *their* children, who taught it to THEIR children, who ... until it finally reached us some forty generations later. But it has reached us in a very different state. Without specialist study, we cannot even begin to understand this kind of English. What has happened?

In brief, English has changed. Many of the words of Old English have disappeared and been replaced by new words. Other words have survived, but have changed either their forms or their meanings so much that we can scarcely recognize them. The grammatical structure of the language has changed enormously. And, though this is hard to see from a written passage, the pronunciation has changed dramatically. Finally, and very obviously, the spelling has changed.

English is in no way unusual. Every language that is spoken by people is constantly changing. If there is one secure lesson that you can take away from reading this book, it is this: languages are always changing.

In this chapter, we shall be looking at some of the ways in which languages change, we shall consider some possible reasons for change, and we shall examine the consequences of change. First, though, let's look more carefully at that piece of Old English.

English a thousand years ago

We'll work through the first sentence of the passage. The word *and*, of course, is just the familiar 'and', though its pronunciation has changed in a way the spelling doesn't show. But *hēo* is harder: it's 'she'. This is just the word *he* with the Old English feminine ending *-o*. This old word survived until recently in northwest England in the form *oo*, but otherwise it has been replaced by a new word *she*, whose origin is probably the Old English *sēo* 'that one' (feminine). The word *cende* means 'gave birth to', past tense of the verb *cennan*. This verb has completely disappeared from the language, but you can at least recognize the ending *-de*, as in *loved* and *walked*. The form *hire* is just about recognizable as 'her'. But *frum-cennedan* is more difficult: the second part is 'born', another form of *cennan*, but *frum-*, which means 'first', has also disappeared. On the other hand, *sunu* is easy: it's 'son', though with a grammatical ending which has long since vanished.

Unexpectedly, *hine* is 'him', and *mid* is 'with', another word which has disappeared, except in the compound 'midwife', literally 'with-woman'. You can probably make out that *cild-clāþum* is 'child-clothes', though both the spellings and the pronunciations have changed: the letter *þ*, called 'thorn', was used in Old English to spell the sounds we now spell *th*. And there's yet another grammatical ending here. The verb *bewand* is simply the modern *wound* with a prefix *be-* which has disappeared in this verb: we no longer have a verb *bewind*. The word *on* is familiar enough, except that we would now say 'in' in this context, for *binne* is just the modern word 'bin', with yet another ending. And *ālegde* is the verb 'laid', with another lost prefix and a spelling that disguises something very close to the modern pronunciation.

The phrase *for þām þe*, literally 'for that that', means 'because', a word which did not exist in Old English. The pronoun *hīe* is 'they', also related to *he*. This word too has disappeared, except for the form *hem* 'them', which still exists in the form written ''em', as in 'Give 'em my regards'. The new forms 'they' and 'them' didn't exist in Old English; they were borrowed from Old Norse, the language of the Vikings, after the Viking settlement and conquest of England not long after this passage was written. The very odd form *næfdon* means '(they) didn't have': it's a contraction of the negative word *ne* 'not' and *hæfdon*, the ordinary past tense of the verb which survives today as 'have'. The form *rūm* 'room' has scarcely changed at all, except in its spelling. The word *cumena* is a form of *cuma* 'guest' showing yet another ending, and *hūs* is recognizable even though 'house' has changed its pronunciation quite noticeably (except in parts of Scotland, where something close to the ancient pronunciation is still in use), and *cumena hūs* is, of course, 'guest house'.

By now you will perhaps have recognized the passage as the beginning of the Christmas story in the Gospel of St Luke. In the familiar King James translation of 1611, this passage runs:

> And she brought forth her firstborn son, and wrapped him in swaddling clothes, and laid him in a manger; because there was no room for them in the inn. And there were in the same country shepherds abiding in the field, keeping watch over their flocks by night. And, lo, the angel of the Lord came upon them, and the glory of the Lord shone round about them; and they were sore afraid.

Among the most striking differences between Old English and modern English are the grammatical ones. You can see that the word order is sometimes different in Old English, and that the words 'a' and 'the' are often missing where modern English requires them (these words were only beginning to come into existence a thousand years ago). But perhaps the most startling difference is the large number of grammatical endings in Old English.

If you have ever studied modern German, you will know that that language displays a depressing abundance of endings. Old English was very much like this: it had three grammatical genders, many different classes of nouns and verbs, and just about as many endings as German. Here is a sample: the Old English forms of *se lange dæg* 'the long day'. Note the change in the vowel of the word for 'day': *æ* is the vowel of *bat*, while *a* is the vowel of *bar* (the overbar marks a long vowel):

	Singular	Plural
Nominative	se lange dæg	þā langan dagas
Genitive	þæs langa dæges	þāra langena daga
Dative	þǣm langan dæge	þǣm langum dagum
Accusative	þone langan dæg	þā langan dagas

But *lang dæg* '(a) long day' had different adjective endings:

Nominative	lang dæg	lange dagas
Genitive	langes dæges	langra daga
Dative	langum dæge	langum dagum
Accusative	langne dæg	lange dagas

In other words, the adjective had two different sets of endings, depending on what kind of word (if any) stood before it. And of course there were many other classes of nouns which took different sets of endings from *dæg*. Aren't you pleased we've managed to get rid of most of this stuff? Even if you're not pleased, all those Italian au pairs and Japanese businessmen who are busily learning English now will surely be delighted that they only have to learn *the long day* and then they're done: there's no agonizing over when to use *langes* or *langum* or *langan*.

But how *did* we get rid of these endings? What happened? Well, there was no one thing that happened. English had been changing since the day the Angles and the Saxons arrived in Britain in about AD 500, and it has naturally carried on changing ever since. Since the Old English grammatical endings could hardly have become much more complicated than they already were, the chances were that any changes that occurred would make the system simpler, and that's what happened. As some endings were lost, there was less reason to retain the other ones, and so more and more endings came to be lost, until we were finally left with no more than the handful of grammatical endings that still survive today: *dog*, *dogs*, *dog's*, *love*, *loves*, *loved*, *loving*, and a few others. Indeed, English has gone so far in this direction that it now has fewer grammatical endings than any other language in Europe, and only a few more than Chinese, which has none at all. It's quite intriguing to reflect that, of all the modern languages of Europe, English is the one which is most like Chinese in its grammar.

And will we finally go all the way, and get rid of all our grammatical endings? We might, but it's impossible to guess. Language change is always with us, but its course is generally unpredictable, and it's quite possible that we might instead start creating some new grammatical endings.

Any of these things is possible. We know that the ancestor of

Chinese had lots of grammatical endings, but the Chinese really did go all the way and get rid of every single one of their endings, so that Chinese today doesn't even have a grammatical distinction between, for example, *dog* and *dogs*, or between *love* and *loved*. On the other hand, Hindi, a major language of India, many centuries ago got rid of a large proportion of its earlier grammatical endings and then invented another bunch of new ones.

Before we leave Old English, it is worth pointing out that the greatest proportion of the grammatical endings were lost in the space of only a few generations during the twelfth and thirteenth centuries. By the beginning of the fourteenth century the endings had become enormously fewer, simpler and more regular. There is perhaps a particular reason for this.

In 1066 England was conquered by the French-speaking Normans, and French became the official language of the country for the next two centuries. French was used for almost all important purposes by the ruling elite, while most people just went ahead and spoke English as they saw fit. There were no ferocious English teachers to rap pupils across the knuckles for using the wrong ending on an adjective, and no English words or forms had any more prestige than any others, since English had no prestige anyway. Anyone who wanted to get ahead concentrated on learning the sort of French used by the Norman nobles and officials; worrying about one's English was a waste of time. Hence there was little resistance to any changes that English speakers might choose to introduce.

In contrast, the grammar of English has changed much less dramatically during the last few hundred years than it did during those two busy centuries, and one of the reasons for this is that English finally deposed French and became the official language of England, with the result that people had to start worrying about speaking the 'right' form of English if they wanted to make a favourable impression in polite society. Once a language becomes prestigious, such worries always tend to inhibit the pace of change to some extent, though they certainly don't prevent changes from occurring, as we shall see below and in Chapter 8.

In fact, of course, English has continued to change constantly throughout its history, and it is still changing today. As a result, the

English of only a few centuries ago is now unrecognizable to us, just as our own English will doubtless be unrecognizable to our descendants a few centuries from now. Changes have occurred and are occurring in every aspect of the language: in grammar, in pronunciation, in vocabulary and in the meanings of words. Let us now look at some of the ways in which languages change, beginning with what is perhaps the most conspicuous kind of change of all.

That's a nice word you've got there – mind if we borrow it?

Something like 60 per cent of the vocabulary of Old English has disappeared, and been replaced by different words. Moreover, the total number of words in English has grown enormously since the Old English period: our vocabulary now contains some hundreds of thousands of words, more than are found in any other language. Where have all these words come from?

Well, there are many ways of obtaining new words, but perhaps the simplest is the process we call **borrowing** – that is, copying the words used in other languages. For most of our history, English-speakers have been enthusiastic borrowers of other people's words.

Even before the ancestral English-speakers arrived in England (see below), they had already borrowed a number of words from Latin, in those days the most prestigious language in Europe, including some words which the Romans themselves had earlier borrowed from Greek. These words have now been in the language so long that only a scholar can be sure they are not native English words: *wine, soap, church, angel, devil, anchor, butter, chalk, cheese, kettle, mile, pound, pepper, street, wall, sack, kitchen* and even *cheap* were all borrowed from Latin more than 1,500 years ago.

When the English-speakers first settled in Britain, that country was already occupied by the Celtic-speakers of British, the direct ancestor of Welsh and Cornish. Only a few Celtic words were taken into English, such as *coomb* 'valley', *brock* 'badger', *dun* 'dark grey', *bin, cross* and of course *druid*, among others. On the other hand, very large numbers of Celtic place names were adopted into English – for example, *Kent, Devon, Cumbria, London, Leeds, York, Dover, Carlisle, Crewe,* and at least the first elements of *Canterbury,*

Aberdeen, *Gloucester*, *Leicester*, *Winchester*, *Lincoln* and *Salisbury*, just to cite a few. Very many British rivers still bear the names given to them by the Celts thousands of years ago: *Thames*, *Trent*, *Severn*, *Wye*, *Avon*, *Calder*, *Dee*, *Derwent*, *Esk*, *Ouse*, *Tees*, *Usk*, and many others.

The Latin-speaking Romans had left Britain not long before the English arrived, but the conversion of the English to Christianity in the seventh century reintroduced Latin into the country, and Latin words began to be borrowed into English in significant numbers: *school*, *rule*, *priest*, *bishop*, *altar*, *master*, *clerk*, *organ*, *tunic*, *circle*, *paper*, *comet*, *crystal*, *temple*, *pear* and *lettuce*, to name a few (again, some of these came originally from Greek).

In the ninth and tenth centuries the Vikings invaded Britain from Scandinavia and settled in large numbers. Their language, which we call Old Norse, was at least partly comprehensible to the English, who did not hesitate to take over hundreds of words from it: *skirt*, *window*, *scrub*, *sky*, *give*, *take*, *get*, *hit*, *kick*, *scatter*, *scrape*, *skill*, *scowl*, *score*, *fellow*, *want*, *skin*, *knife*, *law*, *happy*, *ugly*, *wrong* and even the pronouns *they* and *them*. These words look very convincingly English, but note that the presence of the cluster *sk* or *sc* usually marks a word as Scandinavian, since native English words don't normally contain it. (My ancestors came to the States from Scotland, but my surname *Trask* shows that I must have some Viking ancestry somewhere: the word *träsk* means a pond or a small lake in Norwegian.) The Vikings also introduced a large number of place names into England, such as *Grimsby*, *Derby*, *Whitby*, *Crosby*, *Rugby*, *Scunthorpe*, *Lowestoft* and *Birkbeck*.

Hence even by the time of the Old English passage at the beginning of the chapter, English had already borrowed some thousands of words from Latin, Celtic and Old Norse, a few of which appear in the passage. But this borrowing was as nothing compared to what was about to happen to English. I have already reminded you that the French-speaking Normans conquered England in 1066, and that French was the official language of the country for the next couple of centuries. By the time the descendants of the Normans gave up French for English some generations later, English had already taken over so many thousands of words from the more prestigious

French that the vocabulary of the language had been utterly transformed.

Understandably in the circumstances, the English borrowed words pertaining to warfare, administration, social organization and law from the Normans: *government, castle, service, attorney, chancellor, crime, court, country, estate, judge, jury, captain, lieutenant, sergeant, soldier, chief, noble, royal, prince, duke, baron.* But they borrowed almost equally heavily in virtually every sphere of human activity: *beef, mutton, veal, roast, fry, boil, stew, fruit, colour, pity, virtue, honour, courage, language, sentence, question, literature, letter, college, fool, horrible, mirror, male, female, dignity, second, gentle, champion, charge, check, chaste* – I could go on like this for some time, but you get the picture. In fact, *picture* is another one – it's practically impossible to get through an English sentence today without using a few of these medieval loans from French. Even our word *face* is Norman French: it replaced the native word *anleth*, which rapidly disappeared from the language.

By around 1400, English had reasserted its dominion over French in England, and the flood of French loans began to slow down to – well, not to a trickle, but to a comparatively modest stream. But we English-speakers have never lost our admiration for things French, and such French words as *soup, police, picnic, amateur, boulevard, connoisseur, crochet, débris, fuselage, garage, risqué, souvenir, savoir-faire, restaurant, menu, repartee, cigarette, nuance, ballet, beret* and *café* have all been borrowed in the last two or three centuries.

But our reduced rate of borrowing from French has been more than compensated for by our non-stop borrowing from most of the other languages on the planet. The English-speaking settlers in North America borrowed a number of words from the local Indian languages, such as *teepee, wigwam, tomahawk, skunk, raccoon, moccasin, totem* and *pemmican*, and of course they took over a large number of place names, including *Massachusetts, Connecticut, Mississippi, Illinois, Michigan, Erie* and *Chicago*. The Spanish and Portuguese settlers to the south borrowed many more words, most of which have found their way into English: *tobacco, hurricane, canoe, hammock, tomato, potato, chocolate, cocoa, maize, barbecue, savannah, tapioca, cayenne, llama, jaguar, coyote,* and the *coca* of both *cocaine* and *Coca-Cola*. Settlers in Australia and New Zealand likewise borrowed *kangaroo, wallaby, boomerang, billabong, wombat, kiwi, koala, budgerigar* and *kauri* (a tree) from the indigenous languages, and of course every rugby fan knows the Maori word *haka*.

British settlers in India borrowed *rajah, curry, nabob, sepoy, coolie, cheroot, bungalow, dungaree, mongoose, punch* (the drink), *sahib, bandana, bangle, cheetah, jungle, pyjamas, thug, cashmere* and, surprisingly perhaps, *shampoo*; those in South Africa borrowed *aardvark, veld, spoor* and *trek* from their Afrikaans-speaking neighbours and *impi* 'war party' and *indaba* 'conference' from the local indigenous languages.

Indeed, it's probably safe to say that, if you can name a language, English has borrowed some words from it. From Dutch we take *boss, dock, reef, brandy, yacht, gin* and *coleslaw*; from Spanish, *bonanza, corral, patio, mosquito, stampede* and *sherry*; from German, *plunder, kindergarten, hamster, waltz, pretzel, poodle, rucksack* and, of course, *lager*; from Italian, *violin, opera, spaghetti, duet, carnival, lagoon, studio* and *umbrella*; from Arabic, *alcohol, algebra, mattress, assassin, harem, sherbet* and *tariff*; from Chinese, *tea, ketchup, ginseng, lichee, typhoon* and *kumquat*; from the languages of the Pacific, *taboo, tattoo* and *ukulele*; from African languages, *yam, banana, banjo, gorilla, voodoo* and possibly that most successful of all English words, *OK* (scholars are still debating the source of this word, but a West African origin seems plausible).

We get *yogurt* from Turkish, *bamboo* from Malay, *steppe* from Russian, *caravan* from Persian, *retsina* from modern Greek, *ski* from Norwegian, *smorgasbord* from Swedish, *coach* from Hungarian, *marmalade* from Portuguese, *cinnamon* from Hebrew, *kibitzer* from Yiddish, *whisky* from Scots Gaelic, *phoney* from Irish and *sauna* from Finnish. Recently we seem to have developed some enthusiasm for Japanese words: to such earlier loans as *geisha, hara-kiri, soya, judo, sukiyaki, sake* and *kimono* we have recently added *karaoke, sumo, basho, tempura* and the remarkable *Walkman*, a trade name constructed in English by the Japanese.

The vast majority of these words, of course, are words for genuinely new things: English-speakers had never seen potatoes, or skis, or yogurt, or boomerangs, before they encountered them overseas and adopted them along with their names, just as an earlier generation had never seen castles or colleges before the Norman invasion, or, an earlier generation still, bishops or lettuce. But this is not the only reason for borrowing words: Old English certainly had words for 'language' and 'female' and 'face', and we could perfectly well have carried on using them, but the much greater prestige of French induced many English-speakers to introduce French words into their speech in the hope of sounding more elegant. This attitude is always with us: French no longer enjoys quite the prestige it once had, but you may perhaps know someone who cannot resist spattering his English speech or writing with such French words and phrases as *au contraire*, *joie de vivre*, *au naturel*, *fin de siècle* and *derrière*.

Slightly different is the case of *perestroika* and *glasnost*. As the recent revolution began to unfold in the former Soviet Union, these Russian words began to appear daily in our newspapers and on our television screens. In fact, they are merely the ordinary Russian words for 'restructuring' and 'openness', and we might readily have used the English words, but we preferred (or at least journalists and commentators preferred) to import the Russian terms, perhaps to indicate that we weren't talking about any old restructuring or openness, but specifically about what was going on in the Soviet Union.

Naturally, English is not the only language that borrows words. All languages do it, and recently lots of languages have been borrowing vast numbers of words from English, a topic we shall return to in Chapter 8.

Before we leave the subject of borrowing, let me just point out that it is possible to 'borrow' words which don't exist in the language you think you're borrowing from. English has 'borrowed' from French the phrase *nom de plume*, meaning 'pen name' – but no such phrase existed in French when we borrowed it: it's an English invention. The French have returned the compliment by 'borrowing' the English word *footing* in the sense of 'jogging' – this time a French invention.

But my favourite example is a story told by the American linguist Charles Hockett, who reports that at least one Filipino father, during the American occupation of the Philippines, named his son *Ababís* – after the patron saint of the United States. But no such saint exists. So what happened?

Well, before the Americans arrived, the Philippines were a Spanish colony, and Spanish was (and is) widely spoken. In Spanish, the word for 'saint', when it occurs in a male saint's name, is *San* – hence all those California place names like San Francisco, San José and San Diego. The Filipino father had noticed that American soldiers, in moments of stress, tended to call upon their saint by exclaiming *San Ababís!* – or something like that.

Most of our aitches are missing

It's not just our vocabulary that's been transformed in the last thousand years: the changes in the pronunciation of English have been every bit as dramatic, if not so easy to detect from written texts. Since we don't have space here to discuss all the major changes in our pronunciation, let's look carefully at just one of them: the fascinating story of English *h*.

In Old English, *h* was a very common consonant, and it could occur in almost any position in a word. Here are some examples, all of them in words which still exist in modern English: *habban* 'have', *hiw* 'colour', *hit* 'it', *heah* 'high', *hehþu* 'height', *behindan* 'behind', *hnutu* 'nut', *hnæppian* '(have a) nap', *hræfn* 'raven', *hring* 'ring', *hlud* 'loud', *hlaf* 'loaf', *hlaford* 'lord', *hlæfdige* 'lady', *hwit* 'white', *hwæt* 'what', *niht* 'night', *beorht* 'bright', *fyrhtan* 'frighten', *leoht* 'light', *tahte* 'taught', *hlæhhan* 'laugh', *ruh* 'rough', *syhð* 'sees', *seah* 'saw' (past tense of 'see') and *þurh* 'through'. The *h* was pronounced in all these words, and it was pronounced very vigorously: it wasn't a soft, smooth *h*; it was a loud, scrapy *h*, rather like the *ch* of German *ach* and *Bach*, the *j* of Spanish *José* and *jota*, the *ch* of Hebrew *chaim* 'life', or the Dutch *g* of *Groningen*. This ancient sound is still preserved today in the Scottish word *loch* 'lake', a word borrowed from Scots Gaelic.

But the story of English *h* is not a success story: instead, it's just the opposite. Already by the Old English period, we believe, *h* had been weakened at the beginning of a word to the faint breathing we associate with *h* today, though the scrapy pronunciation was still used in other positions. But that was only the beginning. Not long after the Norman Conquest, English speakers began doing something which the fierce English teachers of the day, had there been any, would have regarded as rather naughty: they began dropping their aitches.

First to go were the aitches that were followed by *l*, *r* and *n*. By the time English began to be written widely again after the conquest, all the words like *loud*, *ring* and *nut* had lost their aitches completely, and not even the fiercest English teachers have ever tried to persuade us to put them back. All the others remained, however, but at this point the spelling conventions of English were changed. First, the sensible old spelling *hw* was replaced by a new form *wh*, so that *hwit* and *hwæt* came to be written as *white* and *what*. Second, the still scrapy aitches in the middles and at the ends of words began to be spelled *gh*: hence the modern spellings like *light*, *bright*, *night*, *laugh*, *rough* and *through*, where *gh* represents an Old English scrapy *h*.

But no sooner had the new spellings become established when the English decided to drop some more aitches. During the fifteenth century, all those scrapy aitches that were spelled *gh* began to be lost from pronunciation; by the sixteenth century only a few rustics and pedants were still pronouncing the aitches in words like *night* and *through*, except in Scotland, where the old pronunciations hung on longer. In a very few words, though, something surprising happened: the scrapy *h* was replaced by an *f*, apparently because the two consonants sound rather similar, and people who were not pronouncing their aitches sometimes misheard the *h* sound as an *f*. That is the reason for the unexpected modern pronunciations like *laugh* and *rough* – originally, they were just mistakes.

The English teachers of the day no doubt complained bitterly about this 'sloppy' dropping of aitches, and I expect a few schoolboyish knuckles got rapped, but to no avail: those aitches got dropped and stayed dropped, and today we have only those useless gee-aitches grinning vacantly at us from words like *night, taught* and *through* to remind us that our ever-so-great-grandparents pronounced aitches in these words more than five hundred years ago.

But the English still weren't done dropping aitches. There are lots of little grammatical words with aitches, like *he*, *him*, *her*, *which*, *why*, *where* and *whether*; these words frequently occur unstressed, and very early they too began to lose their aitches when unstressed, though not when stressed. This variation has been with us for centuries, and even today most educated speakers say (but don't write) things like *What did 'e give 'er?* The pronoun *hit*, which is almost always unstressed, lost its *h* completely: for centuries now, *it* has been the only possible form.

Next to go were the aitches in all other unstressed syllables. No educated speaker has pronounced the *h* in *vehicle* or *annihilate* for generations, and, in the USA at least, pronouncing the *h* in the first word immediately marks you as an uneducated country bumpkin trying to talk proper. But, when the unstressed syllable comes at the beginning of a word, we have had trouble making up our minds. Such words as *historical* and *hotel* have often lost their aitches, producing *'istorical* and *'otel*, and hence such forms as *an historical event* and *an hotel*, but here the aitches have made a kind of stand, and most careful speakers now say *a historical novel* and *a hotel*, with aitches.

In the nineteenth century, the aitches began to disappear from all the words beginning with *hw-* (spelled *wh-*, of course), at least in England. Today even the most careful speakers in England pronounce *which* just like *witch*, *whales* just like *Wales*, and *whine* just like *wine*. There is still, however, a kind of dim folk memory that the pronunciation with *h* is more elegant, and I believe there are still a few teachers of elocution in England who try to teach their clients to say *hwich* and *hwales*, but such pronunciations are now a quaint affectation in England.

But, while careful speakers were dithering about this, most of the rest of the population of England were getting on with some serious *h*-dropping. Specifically, some speakers began dropping *all* their aitches, and pronouncing no aitches at all, making *hair* identical with *air*, *hear* identical with *ear* and *harm* identical with *arm*. There is clear evidence that this type of pronunciation has been in existence for centuries – for example, Shakespeare and Marlowe were making jokes about it in the sixteenth century – and the British linguist James Milroy thinks that such pronunciations may have been in use since the early Middle Ages.

In fact, though educated speakers in England tend to be only

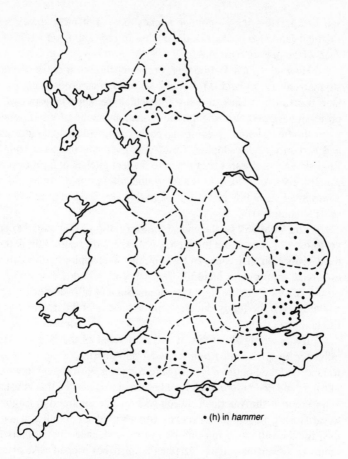

• (h) in *hammer*

FIGURE 5.1 The *h*-pronouncing areas of England
Source: Reprinted with permission from J. Milroy (1992) *Linguistic Variation and Change*, Oxford: Blackwell, p. 138.

dimly aware of the fact, *the vast majority of speakers in England now have no aitches at all*. The map in Figure 5.1 (compiled in the 1960s) shows that aitches survive in vernacular speech only in three small areas of England, and even this map is probably too generous – Norwich, for example, is shown as *h*-ful, but in fact hardly any speakers in Norwich pronounce aitches today. For most speakers in England (and also in Wales), the aitches in *hair* and *head* are just as dead as the ones in *light* and *loud*.

However, such *h*-dropping, prevalent though it is, is strongly stigmatized in England. Middle-class speakers carefully hang on to their remaining aitches, and any vernacular speaker who aspires to a professional career will acquire those precious aitches, for in England today, nothing, *nothing*, stamps a speaker as uneducated so instantly and certainly as *h*-dropping. Mind you, even the most determined English teacher doesn't try to restore the lost aitches in *light* or *it*, or usually even in *which* – it's only the aitches that were still in widespread use a few generations ago that you need to pronounce in order to sound posh.

And what will be the end of the story of *h* in England? No one yet knows, of course, but my money is on the *h*-droppers: I think they have history on their side, and I think that *h*-dropping will continue to spread, until only a handful of elderly fuddy-duddies continue to pronounce their aitches, to the great amusement of everybody else – and then even the fuddy-duddies will be gone, and the last aitches in England with them.

If I'm wrong about this, it will be because of the ever-growing influence of American English. In North America, as in Scotland, Ireland, and the Southern Hemisphere countries, *h*-dropping in words like *hair* and *head* is completely unknown, and it may be that constant exposure to *h*-ful American speech will reverse the trend in England toward losing the remaining aitches. But it's hard to be confident about this, for the following reason. Two or three decades ago, American linguists noticed that aitches were beginning to be dropped in American speech in the *wh-* words like *where* and *whine*. They identified three widely separated parts of the country where this *h*-dropping was going on at the time. But this particular type of *h*-dropping has since spread across the country with astounding speed: the American linguist William Bright recently reported that the aitches are pronounced in *where* and *whine* only by a handful of old fogies. This new style has even reached the remote valleys of Cattaraugus County, where I come from: while I pronounce my aitches in these words, my two younger brothers do not.

At present there is still no sign of *h*-dropping in American English in words like *hair* and *head*, but I wouldn't be at all surprised to see an article in a linguistics journal in a few years' time reporting that *h*-dropping has appeared in these words too in Albuquerque or Duluth or Chattanooga.

The story of *h* illustrates a number of important points about the way in which language change typically proceeds.

1 *A change may at first affect only certain cases, and then spread gradually to other cases.* The loss of English *h* happened at first only before *l*, *r* and *n*, then spread to all aitches except those followed by a vowel or *w*, then spread to aitches in unstressed syllables, then spread to aitches followed by *w*, and finally spread to all remaining aitches.

2 *A change spreads out gradually over a geographical area.* The map in Figure 5.1 shows clearly that the last stage of *h*-dropping in England has spread out from some original area or areas until it has occupied most of England, leaving just three widely separated **relic areas** (as they are called) to which the change has not yet spread. The information from Norwich shows that the spread of *h*-dropping is still continuing, and the information from the USA shows that *h*-dropping in *wh*- words has spread out rapidly from three separate sources.

3 *A change may at first affect the speech of only some speakers in a community and may then spread to other speakers; during this time, the innovation may be stigmatized.* This very common state of affairs is called by linguists **change from below**: an innovation appears in non-prestigious speech varieties and is at first condemned by other speakers; with time, the innovation spreads upward through the social strata until it perhaps becomes accepted as the norm, with the older form then being stigmatized in its turn. This is apparently what has been happening with *h*-dropping: recall that the dropping of *h* in words like *light* was resisted by pedantic speakers but none the less became the norm, while the loss of *h* in *wh*- words was doubtless considered vulgar at first but is now the educated standard in England.

A similar case which has gone further than *h*-dropping is

r-dropping. A couple of centuries ago, some speakers in England began to drop all their *r*s which were not followed by vowels, so that *farther* became identical to *father* and *pore* became identical to *paw*. For a long time, this *r*-dropping was condemned as 'ignorant', but it none the less spread upward until it became the norm in England. Now such *r*-dropping is considered elegant in England, and those speakers in the West Country who still pronounce all their *r*s are considered quaint and rustic – just as I've suggested that *h*-pronouncers will in the future be considered quaint and rustic.

4 *A change which is in progress shows up as variation.* The current variation between *h*-ful and *h*-less types of speech is clearly a consequence of the disappearance of aitches which has been going on in English for centuries. Many of the examples of variation discussed in Chapter 4 also exemplify changes in progress.

In sum, then, we can hear the language changing in front of our ears, though we may not always recognize that what we're hearing is a change in progress. A change which is spread out over many generations, such as the loss of *h* in English, is an instance of what linguists call **drift**: the curious tendency of a language to keep changing in the same direction. Both slow, long-term changes like the loss of *h* and comparatively sudden changes like the acquisition of new words must eventually have profound consequences, and to these consequences we now turn.

Where did English come from?

When the Anglo-Saxons first settled in England some 1,500 years ago, there were already, of course, some regional differences in their speech, though these were not dramatic. With the passage of time, however, further differences began to accumulate. We have seen that an innovation that occurs in one area may spread to a larger area, but that it doesn't necessarily spread to the whole area occupied by the language (recall the dialect maps in Chapter 4). After some centuries, every area of England had undergone some changes in grammar, vocabulary and pronunciation, but failed to undergo other changes that had affected different areas. Consequently, the English-speaking area gradually broke up into a number of regions all distinguished by an ever-greater number of differences – the regional dialects that we considered in the last chapter. By about the year 1500 or so (a thousand years after the settlement), it is clear, speakers from different regions were often finding it very difficult to understand one another.

These regional differences are still with us and they are very familiar. Not long ago there was a striking example of the extent to which English has diverged: a television company put out a programme filmed in the English city of Newcastle, where the local variety of English is famously divergent and difficult, and the televised version was accompanied by *English subtitles*! The producers were afraid that other speakers would be quite unable to understand the 'Geordie' speech of the performers. This ruffled quite a few feathers in Newcastle, but the producers had a point: I recall that, the first time I met a Geordie speaker, it was some days before I could understand a single word he was saying.

As we shall see, the combination of language change with geographical separation is a powerful one, and, in the case of English, the degree of separation was greatly increased by the settlement by English-speakers of North America in the seventeenth century and of Australia and New Zealand in the nineteenth. Already the speech of North America is noticeably different from anything heard in Britain, and the English of, say, Mississippi or North Carolina can be exceedingly difficult for a Briton to understand. Indeed, it is reported that, when American films with soundtracks were first shown in Britain in the 1930s, British audiences, having had almost no previous exposure to American speech, often found them very difficult to understand.

If nothing were to intervene, what do you suppose the result of this growing divergence would be? Easy: eventually the regional varieties of English would diverge so far as to become mutually incomprehensible, and we would be forced to speak, not of dialects, but of separate languages.

It is possible that this will not happen now, thanks to the dramatic advances in transport and communications we have seen in the twentieth century, but it would have happened otherwise. And there is no doubt at all that such breaking up of a single language into several quite different languages has happened uncountably many times before. Indeed, that's exactly how English came into existence in the first place.

More than 1,500 years ago, when most of Britain was still occupied by the language that would eventually develop into Welsh and Cornish, the ancestor of English was spoken on the North Sea coast of the European continent, in areas that are now part of the Netherlands, Germany and Denmark. If the speakers of that language gave it a name, it has not survived: for convenience, we call it **Ingvaeonic**. And it was some of the Ingvaeonic-speaking tribes, including the Angles and the Saxons, who moved across the North Sea into Britain 1,500 years ago. But not *all* of them emigrated: many of them stayed behind in Europe. So what happened to *their* Ingvaeonic? It certainly didn't turn into English.

Of course not, but it did turn into something else, or rather several something elses. The Angles and Saxons took to Britain the same Ingvaeonic speech they were leaving behind, but the North Sea proved to be a formidable barrier to further contact. Ingvaeonic continued to change, but changes occurring on one side of the sea almost never crossed over to the other side, and within a few centuries the insular varieties that we now call English were already sharply different from the continental varieties. And, whereas England gradually came to be united under a single political authority (a factor which to some extent helped to slow the fragmentation of English), the stay-at-homes on the Continent found their territory criss-crossed by political boundaries. Eventually continental Ingvaeonic broke up into several regional varieties which were not even comprehensible to one another, let alone with English. Today linguists recognize three continental languages derived from Ingvaeonic: Dutch, Frisian and Low German (in fact, only some dialects of Dutch and of Low German derive from Ingvaeonic – the linguistic position was really somewhat complicated in this part of the world).

Dutch is spoken in the Netherlands, in half of Belgium and in a small area of northern France around Dunkirk; like English, it has splintered into a number of regional dialects, and a speaker from Amsterdam cannot understand the local Dutch of western Belgium or France (these regional varieties of Dutch are sometimes called

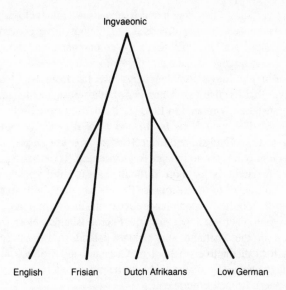

FIGURE 5.2 The Ingvaeonic family tree

Flemish). Frisian was formerly spoken in much of the Netherlands and is still spoken on several islands off the coast of the Netherlands and Germany, and in one corner of the continent. Frisian too has broken up into at least two major dialect groups which are not very similar. Low German is spoken over a wide area of northern Germany, again in a number of quite different varieties. (There is one more modern descendant of Ingvaeonic, but it's not spoken in Europe: it's Afrikaans, a distinctive offshoot of the Dutch introduced into South Africa three centuries ago.)

English-speakers have not been able to understand these languages for many centuries, but we can still recognize tantalizing fragments of our common ancestry. What do you make of such Dutch phrases as *een goed boek* or *koud water* or *de open deur* or *een gouden ring*? Or how about a whole sentence: *Wat wilt u – een kopje koffie of een glas bier*?

We can represent the common ancestry of the Ingvaeonic group of languages by using a **tree diagram**, as in Figure 5.2. The structure of this tree shows that Dutch and Afrikaans are much closer than the other languages, having diverged only about three centuries ago. These languages are still mutually comprehensible, though each sounds very strange to speakers of the other.

But the Ingvaeonic languages are far from being the only relatives that English has. A number of other European languages are also transparently related to English, if not quite so closely. German sentences like *Mein Haus ist alt* and *Dies Wein ist gut* are not so different from English, and even Swedish *Nils har en penna och en bok* you may be able to recognize as meaning 'Nick has a pen and a book'. Icelandic is far more difficult, but, if I tell you that *Fólkið segir, að hún sé lík Anna* means 'People say that she is like Anna', you will spot the resemblance. Also in this group are Danish, Norwegian, Faeroese (spoken in the Faeroe Islands), Norn (formerly spoken in the Shetland and Orkney Islands north of Scotland), Yiddish (a distinctive offshoot of German) and Gothic (an extinct language spoken by many of the barbarian invaders who overthrew the western Roman Empire).

These languages are called the **Germanic** languages, and they all started off millennia ago as nothing more than dialects of a single language, which we call **Proto-Germanic**. The Germanic family tree is shown in Figure 5.3.

Who spoke Proto-Germanic, and where and when? This is not a simple question, since the Proto-Germanic speakers were illiterate and left no written texts behind. But the consensus of scholars is that the language was probably spoken in southern Scandinavia around 500 BC, and that groups of Germanic speakers spread from there into northern, eastern and southern Europe, and finally, a thousand years later, into Britain. The dialects spoken by these groups have diverged into a number of distinct languages, but the relatedness of these languages is still easy to see.

And Proto-Germanic is not the end of the story, or rather it is not the beginning. Two hundred years of careful research has demonstrated beyond any doubt that Proto-Germanic itself began life as a dialect of a still more ancient language, and that the Germanic languages are thus related to a vast family of languages spoken over most of Europe and much of Asia. This enormous family includes the

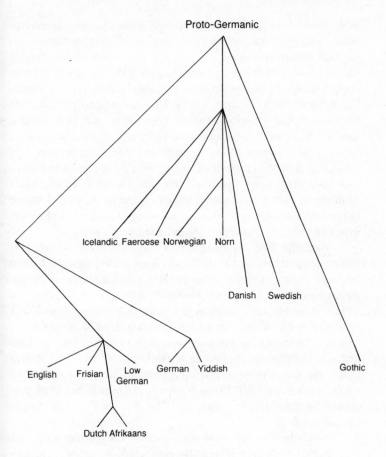

FIGURE 5.3 The Germanic family tree

Celtic languages like Irish and Welsh, the Romance languages like French, Spanish and Italian, the Slavic languages like Russian, Polish and Serbo-Croatian, the Baltic languages like Lithuanian, several rather isolated languages like Greek, Albanian and Armenian, the Iranian languages like Persian and Kurdish, the north Indian languages like Hindi, Panjabi, Bengali and Gujarati, and a number of now extinct languages formerly spoken in the Balkans, in modern Turkey and in central Asia. We call it the **Indo-European** family, and the Indo-European languages are, of course, descended from a remote ancestor called **Proto-Indo-European**, or **PIE**. We think PIE was spoken around 6,000 years ago, probably somewhere in eastern Europe, possibly in southern Russia, by a group of people who rode horses and had wheeled vehicles, agriculture and domesticated animals. We know this because such PIE words as those for 'horse', 'wheel', 'axle', 'grain', 'cow', 'sheep' and 'dog' have survived in a number of daughter languages. For example, we're confident that the PIE word for 'sheep' was *owis* (the asterisk marks an unattested form reconstructed by linguists) because of the existence of Sanskrit (an ancient language of India) *avis*, Latin *ovis*, Greek *ois*, Lithuanian *avis*, Old Irish *oi*, all meaning 'sheep', and English *ewe*.

Naturally, PIE must itself have been descended from a still earlier ancestor, and so on, all the way back to the origins of human language perhaps 100,000 years or more ago, but it is exceedingly difficult to trace things back further into the past: eventually the weight of accumulated changes in languages becomes so great that we can no longer identify an ancient common origin with confidence – though a number of linguists are working very hard on this problem, and some of them are beginning to think that we might be able to derive the Indo-European and other families from a very remote ancestor which they call **Proto-Nostratic** and which they think was spoken perhaps 15,000 years ago. But this idea is still deeply controversial.

None the less, we have succeeded in tracing the origins of English back to an unidentified, illiterate people living somewhere in eastern Europe around 6,000 years ago. These people gradually spread out over much of Asia and Europe, and one group moved first into Scandinavia, then south into much of Europe. Some of these eventually crossed the North Sea into Britain, where their Germanic language, eventually called English, became in turn the national language of England, the language of the British Empire, and finally the most influential and widely used language in the world.

Further reading

There are many excellent books on the history of English; some of the better ones are Baugh and Cable (1993), Pyles (1971), Strang (1970), Barber (1993) and Williams (1975). Rather different is the book by McCrum *et al.* (1992), which concentrates on social factors in the history of English. There are also many books on the history of English words: Manser (1988) is a light-hearted one, while Sheard (1966), though drier, is much more detailed. For language change generally, the best introductions are Trask (1994), which is very elementary, and Aitchison (1991); more substantial texts include McMahon (1994), Crowley (1992) and Lehmann (1992). The relation between variation and change, including the story of *h*, is discussed in Milroy (1992). Bauer (1994) is an introductory book describing the changes going on right now in standard English. Among the better introductions to the Indo-European family are Lockwood (1969 and 1972).

Chapter 6

Language, mind and brain

In Chapter 1 I pointed out the crucial importance of our peculiar vocal tract in allowing us to speak. But, along with that vocal tract, our ancestors also evolved something else that appears to be essential for using language: our large brain. For millions of years, even after they had learned to walk upright, our ancestors made do with small ape-like brains – then suddenly, almost overnight in evolutionary terms, our brains quadrupled in size. No one knows just why this happened, but there is no shortage of speculations – and the favourite speculation is that our brains were developing specifically to allow us to use language.

Whether this guess is right or not, there has naturally been intense interest in finding out how and where language is organized inside the brain. The pursuit of **neurolinguistics** (the study of the relation between language and brain) has never been easy, however. Until recently, there was no direct way of examining the functioning of a normal, healthy brain, and the only way of extracting information was to

study the speech of those unfortunate individuals who had suffered brain damage and then, after their deaths, to perform a post-mortem in order to see which parts of the brain had been damaged. As someone has remarked, this is rather like trying to find out how a television set works by examining nothing but smashed sets. Nevertheless, neurolinguists have managed to learn a good deal by using this approach.

Damaged brain, disordered speech

The brain can suffer damage in a variety of ways: a blow to the head, a wound in the head, partial suffocation, or, most familiarly perhaps, a stroke. The brain consumes fully one-quarter of our oxygen intake, and, if a blood clot gets trapped in the small blood vessels of the brain, the surrounding tissues will quickly die of suffocation. The effects of such damage are highly unpredictable, but often terrible, and one of the commonest results is some kind of disruption of the victim's ability to use language. Disordered language resulting from brain damage has usually been called **aphasia**, but, since this term means literally 'absence of speech', and since few if any sufferers lose their linguistic ability entirely, many neurolinguists now prefer the term **dysphasia**, which means 'disordered speech'.

In the first half of the nineteenth century several researchers independently noticed that a number of brain-damaged patients were turning up with strikingly similar disorders of speech, and that all of these victims, upon post-mortem, proved to have suffered damage to roughly the same area of the brain. In 1864 the French surgeon Paul Broca finally announced his findings with eight such patients. The disorder that he described is now known as **Broca's aphasia**, and the area of the brain that he identified is called **Broca's area**. With a high degree of consistency, it seems, damage to Broca's area produces the symptoms of Broca's aphasia.

Broca's area of the brain is a small patch, not much more than an inch across, of the *cerebral cortex* (the wrinkly grey outer surface of the cerebrum, the large, walnut-shaped part of the brain). If you put your finger to your head just above your left temple, you'll be pointing at Broca's area – for Broca's area, in the vast majority of people, is on the *left* side of the brain.

Damage to Broca's area typically produces a highly specific and readily identifiable type of aphasia. The victim's speech becomes painfully slow and laborious – every individual word has to be squeezed out with tremendous effort. Naturally, the ordinary rhythm of speech is destroyed, and so is the ordinary intonation. Most striking of all, though, is the grammar: there isn't any. Broca's aphasics are unable to construct grammatical sentences. They lose most of those little grammatical words like *of*, *the*, *to*, *if*, *be* and *or* (though they retain homophonous words like *bee* and *oar*!), and they usually lose the grammatical markings on words, such as plurals, past tenses and the *-ing* that goes on verb forms. Indeed, Broca's aphasics can hardly produce any verbs: most of the words they squeeze out so painfully are nouns. Finally, their articulation is poor: their pronunciation is slurred and sometimes hard to interpret. Here is a sample of the speech produced by a Broca's aphasic, who has just been asked what brought him to the hospital:

> Yes – ah – Monday ah – Dad – and Dad – ah – hospital – and ah – Wednesday – Wednesday – nine o'clock and ah Thursday – ten o'clock ah doctors – two – two – ah doctors and – ah – teeth – yah. And a doctor – ah girl – and gums, and I.

In spite of its laboured nature, the speech of a Broca's aphasic usually makes a reasonable amount of sense. Moreover, such patients usually understand what is said to them, except that they have trouble with grammatically complex sentences like *The boy who was kissed by the girl cried*. They can usually read, but they have great difficulty reading regular inflected forms like *dogs* and *wanted* – though interestingly they cope much better with irregular inflections like *children* and *took*. Further, they are always painfully aware that they are having difficulty in speaking. Perhaps partly because of this, Broca's aphasics often respond to treatment: they can hardly ever be cured, but often they show substantial improvement over time.

Very different is a second type of aphasia identified by the German investigator Carl Wernicke in 1874, and now known as **Wernicke's aphasia**. The speech of Wernicke's aphasics is very rapid and fluent – indeed, it often seems to come out in a breathless rush. Rhythm and intonation are fairly normal, and most of the ordinary grammatical structure is intact. In fact, if you listen casually to the speech of such a patient without paying much attention, you might even fail to notice that anything was wrong. But, as soon as you listen carefully, you will notice the big problem that Wernicke's aphasics have: what they say makes no sense. There may be short sequences that make sense in isolation, but these are strung together in a meaningless way, and often broken up by nonsense words. Here is a sample:

> If I could I would. Oh, I'm taking the word the wrong way to say, all the barbers here whenever they stop you it's going around and around, if you know what I mean, that is tying and tying for repucer ... repuceration, well, we were trying the best that we could while another time it was with the beds over there ...

Wernicke's aphasics also have severe difficulty with comprehension: they understand little or nothing of what is said to them. Moreover, they seem quite unaware that they are having difficulties, and frequently become annoyed or frustrated when others seem unable to understand what they are saying. Naturally, it's hard to treat someone who doesn't know he has a problem, and Wernicke's aphasics rarely respond to treatment.

Like Broca, Wernicke was able to identify a particular area of the brain that had been damaged in patients showing such symptoms. **Wernicke's area**, slightly larger than Broca's area, is also on the left side of the cerebral cortex in most people: if you put your finger just above and slightly behind your left ear, you'll be pointing at it.

Now damage to Wernicke's area largely destroys comprehension and severely impairs access to vocabulary. Damage to Broca's area, in contrast, destroys grammatical structure and impairs the production of speech. Other research has shown that Broca's area is fairly close to the *motor area* of the brain, which controls muscular movements, while Wernicke's area lies just behind the *auditory area*, which seems to be responsible for processing input from the ears. All this suggests an obvious organization of language in the brain. The auditory area takes input from the ears and sends it on to Wernicke's area, which is responsible for comprehension. In speaking, Wernicke's area, which has access to ordinary vocabulary, sends the words to Broca's area, which provides the required grammatical structure, including all the grammatical words and affixes, and then passes its instructions on to the motor area, which directs the muscles of the vocal organs to produce the required output.

This view, which we can call the *standard model*, clearly requires the existence of a connection between Wernicke's and Broca's areas, and Broca himself early predicted that such a connection would be found, and that specific damage to this connection would produce yet another type of aphasia. The connection was duly found: just below the surface of the brain, a J-shaped bundle of fibres impressively called the *arcuate fasciculus* connects Wernicke's area directly to Broca's area. Damage to this connection causes **conduction aphasia**, in which the sufferer shows many of the same symptoms as a Wernicke's aphasic, but retains good comprehension, with the added twist that he is incapable of repeating anything said to him. This outcome is entirely what the standard model predicts: Wernicke's area is simply unable to 'talk' to Broca's area, and hence unable to 'tell' it what it has just heard.

In the very rare **isolation aphasia**, a freakish injury leaves the language areas intact but totally disconnected from the rest of the brain. The victim can neither understand speech nor speak spontaneously, apart from a few conventional phrases and some childish verses, but tends to repeat mechanically anything said by someone else, though she retains the ability to sing songs and even to learn new songs.

A crucial fact about aphasia is that it affects users of sign language exactly like users of spoken language. A signer with Broca's aphasia signs slowly and leaves out all or most of the grammatical inflections (remember that sign languages like ASL and BSL have *lots* of grammar, just like any spoken language). A signer with Wernicke's aphasia signs rapidly and fluently but makes little sense, and also has great difficulty in understanding other people's signs. And all aphasic signers who are not physically paralysed can use their hands normally for other purposes, including non-linguistic gestures like pointing and waving. This evidence shows indisputably that what

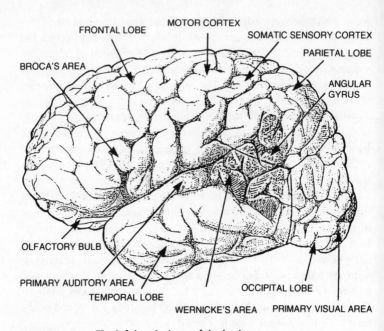

FIGURE 6.1 The left hemisphere of the brain

Source: Reprinted with permission from N. Geschwind (1979) 'Specializations of the human brain', *Scientific American* (international edn, September), p. 161, drawn by Carol Donner.

the language areas control is *language*, and not merely the use of the vocal tract or of the ears.

Figure 6.1 shows a diagram of the left hemisphere with the language areas and others demarcated according to the standard model.

The standard model has proved to be rather successful at accounting for the observed consequences of brain damage. Of course, no two victims of aphasia ever suffer exactly the same brain damage, and no victim ever sustains damage exclusively in one neatly defined area of the brain, and hence individual aphasics in practice exhibit a wide variety of symptoms. Moreover, some very recent research has considerably muddied the waters by apparently demonstrating that, in many people, the two language areas are not located just where they're 'supposed' to be, but are often some distance away, or even smeared out instead of precisely delineated. On the other hand, we now have techniques for watching what's going on inside the brain of a normal, healthy, conscious person, particularly the PET scanner (for *positron emission tomography*); this technique confirms that the familiar language areas indeed exist and are particularly active when the subject is performing a linguistic task, such as listening, speaking or reading.

Perhaps the most unexpected complication of the standard model, though, is one that was discovered long ago: while most people have their language areas on the left side of the brain, about 3 per cent have these areas instead on the *right* side, or rarely even on *both* sides. Interestingly, almost all such people are left-handed (or ambidextrous), though fully 85 per cent of left-handed people have their language areas on the left side. It is hard to know what to make of this, but let us now turn to a more detailed consideration of left–right asymmetries in the brain.

Left versus right

The cerebrum of the human brain, in which most of our higher cognitive faculties appear to be located, is divided into two symmetric halves called *hemispheres*; these hemispheres are connected only by a small, hard bundle of tissue called the *corpus callosum*. It was discovered long ago that each hemisphere is responsible for one half of the body, but, because our remote ancestors somehow contrived to evolve a 180° twist between the spinal cord and the brain, it is the left hemisphere of the brain which looks after the right side of the body, and vice versa. Hence, apart from possible aphasia, damage to the left hemisphere can produce such consequences as blindness in the right eye, deafness in the right ear, or paralysis of the right side of the body.

Language is not the only faculty located in the left hemisphere. In general, most of our analytical abilities appear to be concentrated there, too, such as the ability to do arithmetic, to solve an algebraic equation, or to decide the chronological order in which things have

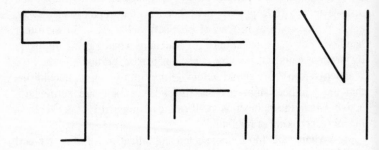

FIGURE 6.2 A right-hemisphere test

happened. Moreover, neurologists have managed to identify a number of well-defined areas in the left hemisphere with specific functions, like the language areas.

The right hemisphere is different. It appears to be more amorphous than the left, and there are few if any well-defined specialist areas in it. But the right hemisphere is the one we primarily rely on for recognition and association. For example, look at Figure 6.2. What do you see? Almost certainly, you immediately perceive an English word. But why? There is in fact no word in the picture – only a jumble of straight lines. However, your right hemisphere has a powerful talent for spotting familiar patterns in just such a jumble of data, and it quickly finds one here. In fact, this is the sort of thing your right hemisphere is doing almost every moment. It sifts the mass of sensory data pouring into the brain and organizes this mass into comprehensible and familiar patterns.

At the moment, as I write, I am enjoying my magnificent view of the university's car park. I can see the expanse of grey asphalt marked with neat white lines, and I recognize it as a car park, as the same car park I see every day, and as the place I have parked my car. I can see two cars (today is Saturday, and things are quiet); I recognize them as cars, and note that neither belongs to anybody I know. Two people have just walked down the steps; I instantly realized that they were a man and a woman and both total strangers to me. Pretty humdrum stuff, apparently – humdrum, but absolutely vital to my existence. It's my right hemisphere that's working all this out for me. What happens when the right hemisphere is damaged?

One of the most famous cases of right-hemisphere damage is that of Dr P., a skilled musician and music teacher who suffered an apparently mild stroke in his right hemisphere. In most respects, the stroke had no visible effects: he remained highly intelligent and cultured, able to speak fluently and elegantly, able to make subtle jokes, able to remember facts, able to play, sing and continue teaching. In fact, he was perfectly normal – except for one thing.

He had lost part of that humdrum ability I have just described. He could no longer assemble his visual data into recognizable patterns, and as a result he could no longer recognize things by looking at them. When an object was placed in his hands, he examined it carefully, and, using his healthy left-hemisphere analytical abilities, announced 'It's about six inches in length ... a convoluted red form with a linear green attachment.' When pressed with the question 'But what do you think it *is*?', he pondered in some perplexity 'Not easy to say ... it lacks the simple symmetry of the Platonic solids, although it may have a higher symmetry of its own.' Instructed to smell the object, he looked puzzled, but politely complied. Suddenly he came to life. 'Beautiful! An early rose!'

Dr P. had lost neither the word *rose* nor the concept of a rose. He had instead lost the humdrum ability to put together a mass of red and green visual impressions into a coherent whole and assign the result to the category of roses. His intact left hemisphere allowed him to construct a careful and detailed description of every part of the object, and to express that description in perfect English – but his damaged right hemisphere could do nothing with the visual data, and hence could not provide a unified concept to the left hemisphere for naming. However, it was only his visual processing that was defective, and as soon as useful non-visual information became available – in this case, smell – his right hemisphere functioned perfectly: Dr P. had no trouble in spotting the familiar smell of a rose and in interpreting what it meant.

One of the most striking and tragic consequences of Dr P.'s disability was his total loss of the ability to recognize faces. Not only could he not recognize even the most familiar faces, he couldn't tell whether something he was looking at was a face or not. When tested with photographs, he failed to recognize almost all the people in the pictures, even his brother, his wife and himself. Occasionally he could get one by spotting one or two particularly distinctive features: for example, by picking out the mane of hair and the bushy moustache, he correctly guessed that one picture was of Albert Einstein. But his disability was profound: Dr P. would pat parking meters on the head, assuming they were children, and try to strike up conversations with carved knobs on furniture, which he had mistaken for faces.

Dr P.'s disability was not specifically linguistic, though of course it had substantial consequences for his ability to use language in the normal way. But the right hemisphere's particular talents sometimes show up linguistically in more direct ways. One of these lies in the expression of emotions: some people with right-hemisphere damage lose the ability to express their emotions – although they can still *feel* emotions – and as a result their speech, though otherwise normal, comes out as flat, lifeless, mechanical, almost robotic, and their faces remain blank, no matter how elated or furious they may feel. And even a victim of unusually severe left-hemisphere damage who has totally lost the faculty of speech can still often sing songs, sometimes very well, and even learn new songs: apparently learning and producing the words of a song is something the right hemisphere handles, or can handle, in spite of its normal linguistic ineptitude. Engagingly, many such people retain the ability to swear like a marine sergeant – apparently the right hemisphere does have *some* vocabulary! (Actually, there is good reason to believe that swearing, like laughing, sobbing and screaming, is not controlled by the cerebral cortex at all, but by some deeper and more ancient part of the brain.)

Fascinatingly, when a user of sign language suffers that right-hemisphere damage which destroys the ability to register ordinary facial expressions, she can none the less *still* make the facial expressions which form a part of the grammar of sign language – demonstrating that the linguistic use of expressions is governed by a different part of the brain from that which handles non-linguistic expressions. Other types of right-hemisphere damage produce the strange disability called *left neglect*: the sufferer, though not technically blind, fails to see anything in the left visual field, fails to draw the left side when drawing pictures, and even fails to dress the left side of her body. But a signer with this impairment still uses the left side of the visual field normally when signing – again showing that the language faculties are largely independent of other, non-linguistic functions of the brain.

The standard model is clearly good enough to take us a long way toward understanding in the brain, but there is a great deal that we are far from understanding. One of the most puzzling problems is the way that words are stored in the brain. We believe that Wernicke's area plays a crucial role in *access* to vocabulary, but that doesn't mean the words themselves are stored in Wernicke's area, and in fact we're pretty sure they're not. A number of fascinating and bewildering cases of language disability reported in the last few years have suggested tantalizing ideas but generally left us feeling more ignorant than ever about what's going on. Most aphasics exhibit some degree of **anomia**, or the inability to find the words for things, and some of them, even with otherwise fairly normal speech, can hardly find any words at all. But certain patients have turned up with startlingly specific versions of anomia almost unaccompanied by any other symptoms. Here is a sample.

Several patients have been reported who have no trouble finding the words for inanimate objects like *chair* and *road* but who cannot find the words for living things such as *woman* and *dog*. Does this mean that we store words for living things in a separate place in our brain? Another man lost nothing but words for fruits and vegetables: he had no trouble of any kind with any other words, but he could not name any fruit or vegetable, whether he was given a verbal description, a picture, or even a real banana or cucumber, and he could not decide whether a particular item that was giving him trouble might be a fruit or a vegetable. It seems almost inconceivable that we should be storing words for fruits and vegetables in a special place, and few linguists would be happy to accept such a conclusion, yet how can we explain what has happened to this patient?

Perhaps the most striking cases are those of two women who

had suffered left-hemisphere strokes. Both women proved to have no trouble with nouns, but to have severe trouble with verbs, *even when the noun and the verb were the same word*. They had no problem in speaking or writing down sentences like *There's milk in the glass* or *That's a nice picture*, in which *milk* and *picture* are nouns, but they couldn't cope with sentences like *She can milk a cow* or *Try to picture the scene*, in which they are verbs. Even when the sentences were dictated to them, and they were asked to write down just the one word, they could write down the noun, but not the identical verb. These findings suggest that nouns and verbs are somehow stored differently in the brain. Such a conclusion is more acceptable to most linguists than special storage arrangements for names of fruits and vegetables, but it still doesn't tell us anything about how any of these words are actually stored: it only tells us that things are complicated.

Even more perplexing are the patients who manage to lose entire languages. Elderly people who have learned several languages earlier in life sometimes, when afflicted with mind-rotting illnesses like Alzheimer's disease, lose one language after another, but they usually retain their mother tongue the longest. But a number of quite young people have turned up who speak two or three languages and who, after some form of brain damage, lose and regain all of their languages, one at a time, in rapid succession. One French Canadian man, bilingual in English, lost his French but kept his English, as a result of which he couldn't speak to his French monoglot wife. After a week, he regained his French but at the same time lost his English, so he couldn't speak to the doctors and nurses in the hospital. In some cases, this sort of thing can go on for months, and no one has any idea how to explain it.

In fact, aphasic patients have been discovered who exhibit almost every conceivable set of symptoms. There are sufferers who can speak but not read, read but not write, write but not read (even what they've just written!). The one conclusion which many specialists are prepared to draw from such bewildering observations is that our language capacity must be in some sense **modular** – that is, it cannot be a formless whole, but rather it must be divided up into a number of specialized subcomponents, each using a different set of neural fibres in the brain. While still controversial, this conclusion is not at all surprising, since we already know that other mental faculties are modular. As is shown by Dr P.'s experience, vision is modular: different parts of the brain handle different aspects of vision. Why should we expect language to be different?

Indeed, we already know for sure that language processing is modular in certain respects. For example, when we hear someone speaking, our brains instantly decompose the speech sounds into at least three components: the identity of the voice, the tone of voice (angry, amused, or whatever) and the strictly linguistic content. Even when you hear a foreign language you don't know, you can recognize individual voices and infer something about the tone, even though you can't process the linguistic part. Clearly our brains must be separating these things out and processing them separately.

The divided self

The terrible disease called *epilepsy* appears to be a kind of electrical storm in the brain: in an epileptic attack, meaningless nervous impulses flood around the brain in such profusion that they over-whelm its ordinary functioning, and the victim loses all control over himself. Quite a few years ago, searching for a way of reducing this flood of nervous activity, surgeons hit upon the idea of cutting through the corpus callosum.

The corpus callosum, you will recall, is the sole connection between the left and right hemispheres of the brain, and cutting it therefore removes all communication between the two hemispheres. But it does, in most cases, confer a great deal of relief upon chronic sufferers from epilepsy, and hence many such sufferers have agreed to undergo the operation, in the hope of being able to lead fairly normal lives, free of the terrifying and destructive epileptic attacks. Relief from the attacks they do get – but what is life like with a divided brain?

Well, it's strange, though at least some of the strangeness makes sense in terms of what we have said about the **lateralization** of the brain – its division into hemispheres with specialized functions.

Suppose an otherwise normal and healthy person with a **split brain** is given a hammer. He can use the hammer normally with either hand. If the hammer is in his right hand, he can understand and obey instructions to do something with the hammer. But, if the hammer is in his left hand, he can't do this. He understands the instructions, all right, and he can explain clearly what he's supposed to do – but he just can't do it. Why?

Well, the language areas are in the left hemisphere, which controls the right hand. So the left hemisphere can interpret the instructions and direct the right hand to do what is required. But the left hand is controlled by the right hemisphere, and, when the corpus callosum has been cut, the left hemisphere has no way of communicating with the right hemisphere, which has no language faculties of its own. So the left hemisphere understands the instructions, but it has no way of getting the word to the left hand. Such results confirm strongly that, in most people, language is indeed located only in the left hemisphere.

In fact, the study of people with split brains has revealed that the right hemisphere is not entirely devoid of linguistic ability. There are simple techniques for presenting words or objects to only one eye or one ear at a time. A split-brain individual has no difficulty in understanding or explaining words presented to the right eye or the right ear (the left hemisphere), but even when it is the left eye or left ear that gets the stimulus, the right hemisphere proves capable of recognizing some dozens of simple words – though that seems to be about it. The linguistic capacity of the right hemisphere is severely limited, but it's not quite zero.

In some other respects, though, the behaviour of split-brain individuals is more unexpected. Most such individuals, on having a pornographic picture shown to the left eye only, blush or giggle – but still cannot describe what they have seen, and typically insist that they have seen nothing at all. One woman reports that she has trouble choosing clothes in the morning, because each of her hands insists on picking out something different to wear. And, when reading a book, she has to sit on one hand, because otherwise that hand keeps trying to turn the page she is reading. This kind of behaviour has fascinated both neurologists and philosophers, because it seems to suggest that each hemisphere of the brain has an identity and a consciousness of its own. Normally, these two consciousnesses are melded into one via the corpus callosum, but, when that connection is gone, the two halves of the brain can go their own separate ways.

Funny things, tongues

Psycholinguistics may be impressively defined as the study of the relation between language and mind. In practice, what psycholinguists chiefly look at is language processing: the details of the procedures by which language is produced and comprehended. Such specialists have developed a battery of techniques for testing what subjects are doing when given various tasks to perform in an experimental setting, but a certain amount of valuable information can also be extracted from spontaneous speech. One of the most fascinating things about spontaneous speech is the occurrence of **slips of the tongue**.

Slips of the tongue, or at least the most familiar types of them, are sometimes called **spoonerisms**, after the Reverend W. A. Spooner of New College, Oxford, who produced so many of them that every amusing slip that anybody ever heard or invented came to be attributed to him. Among the things he is alleged to have come out with are (in a sermon) *The Lord is a shoving leopard*, (in church) *Mardon me, Padam, but this pie is occupewed*, and (to a negligent student) *You have hissed all my mystery lectures and tasted the whole worm*.

Some of these are doubtless apocryphal, but everybody commits a slip of the tongue now and again. We say *bred and bekfast* instead of *bed and breakfast*, or *budbegs* instead of *bedbugs*, or *He was eaten by missionaries* instead of *He was eaten by cannibals* (this is another one of Spooner's), or *Has the dog been eaten?* (a blend of *Has the dog eaten?* and *Has the dog been fed?*). Study of such slips has revealed a number of interesting patterns which shed some light on the way our minds construct utterances.

One of the most obvious findings is that, when speech sounds are inadvertently rearranged, the output always conforms to the ordinary rules for combining consonants and vowels. So *slips of the tongue*, for example, might possibly come out as *tips of the slongue*, but never as *tlips of the songue*, because English words cannot begin with the cluster *tl-*. Similarly, *fingerprint* might come out as *pingerprint* or *pingerfrint* or perhaps even as *pringerfint*, but never as *pfinger-rint*, since the cluster *pf-* can't begin English words either.

Similarly, transposed words are nearly always of the same grammatical category. People say things like *He threw the window out the clock*, with transposed nouns, or *Please wash the table and clear the dishes*, with transposed verbs, but almost never things like *He clocked the throw out the window*, with noun and verb transposed.

A third finding is that, when words are simply replaced by other words, the word used is often closely related in meaning to the intended one. Hence we find frequent cases like *Her marriage broke up an hour and a half ago* (intended *a year and a half ago*) and *I really like to get up in the morning* (intended *I really hate . . .*).

Yet another finding is that slips of the tongue are more frequent when the result involves (misplaced) real words than when it involves nonsense words: hence *rare bug* (for *bear rug*) is more likely to be heard than *tinner dable* (for *dinner table*). Simple substitutions almost always involve real words: *first and girl to go* (intended *first and goal to go*, an expression from American football).

There is, of course, a celebrated view, developed by the psychoanalyst Freud, that such slips tend to reveal the underlying anxieties of the speaker, often especially sexual ones. A modest amount of largely anecdotal evidence might be thought to support this, such as the occasion on which a male professor, advising an attractive female student on her thesis, was heard to say *It needs orgasmic unity* (intended *organic unity*). There has even been an experiment showing that, when male university students were asked to perform a carefully designed reading test administered by an attractive woman who was 'provocatively dressed' (details not supplied, but presumably she was wearing rather less than a white lab coat), they produced a much higher than normal proportion of sexually charged slips, such as *fast passion* for *past fashion*. The vast majority of recorded slips, however, show nothing of this sort, but only a degree of misfiring of the speech-producing apparatus.

What is striking about slips of the tongue is the extent to which they preserve linguistic structure. Even the most dramatic examples tend to do this, like the comment, made by a speaker introducing an

American political candidate, that he was *as American as mother pie and applehood*, or like the mother who told her young child *Brush your bed* (intending *Brush your teeth and make your bed*). This suggests to some investigators that our brains might contain some kind of 'editor', which checks impending utterances for linguistic integrity. Once again, though, I have to report that no one really knows.

Another very familiar problem of speaking is the **tip-of-the-tongue phenomenon**. We all have this experience from time to time: we're happily speaking along, and all of a sudden we want a particular word or name, and we just can't find it. It happened to me recently when I was trying to remember the surname of my editor: I knew the name was short, only four of five letters, and probably only one syllable, but for some moments I could only blunder along, starting with the dismal *Evans* and *Jones*, then working through the more promising *Dell* and *Hill*, before the right name suddenly popped into my head: *Hall*.

I will confess at once that virtually nothing is known about why this happens: for some mysterious reason, our normally reliable and lightning-quick machinery for finding words just stalls on some particular item, and that lost item can only be located by making an extraordinary effort (if even then). But what is particularly interesting about the tip-of-the-tongue phenomenon is the way that effort proceeds.

In my case, all I could remember was that the name was very short and probably only one syllable. Study of the phenomenon, however, has revealed that speakers searching for a lost word can dredge up the most amazing information about it without actually finding it. Again, you will be familiar with this: 'I'm sure it has an *m* in it somewhere.' As in my case, we can often recall the approximate length of the word, perhaps even the precise number of syllables; just as often we can remember that it contains some particular sounds or letters, and sometimes we can recover whole syllables. Interestingly, there is clear evidence that the beginnings and endings of lost words are recalled much more readily than their middles, a phenomenon which some psycholinguists have dubbed the **bathtub effect**, because it reminds them of someone lying in the bath with only head and feet

135

sticking out of the water (my personal view is that psycholinguists must take some pretty interesting baths). The person looking for *Belker* who came up with *Bender* illustrates this tendency perfectly, as does the search for *silicosis* which yielded *psittacosis* (another disease, as it happens).

But almost *any* resemblance or connection may induce a wrong guess. Trying to find the adjective *articulate* once, I successively produced *loquacious*, *garrulous*, *glib* and *verbose*: all adjectives of related meaning. Someone looking for *Slaughterhouse Five* came up with *Fahrenheit 451* (another book title ending in a number); a search for *Olivia Hussey* yielded *Olivia de Havilland* (another actress called *Olivia*); the loss of *Delphi* induced *Mecca* (another city to which people make pilgrimages). The linguist Paul Schachter, searching for *Olivia Newton-John*, tried *Harriet Beecher Stowe* and *Edna May Oliver* (women with three-word names) and, fascinatingly, *Debbie Harry* and *Helen George* (women whose surname is a man's given name). In this last case, it was only upon reflection afterward that Schachter spotted the connection *John ~ Harry ~ George*, but apparently his subconscious brain was actively looking for such a name.

Data like these are clearly telling us something about the way in which vocabulary is stored in the brain and retrieved when required. It looks very much as though our brains do not simply file words away like so many bottles of wine in a wine cellar. Rather, it appears that words are stored with innumerable links to other words: links to words of similar sound or spelling, of related meaning, of the same grammatical class, or having almost any conceivable connection in terms of our experience and our knowledge of the world. Schachter's experience suggests that such unexpected links as 'women whose surnames are men's given names' actually exist within our brains. We may have little idea what to make of these observations at present, but they certainly are interesting and suggestive. But these unexpected links are as nothing compared to some other unexpected links which have turned up.

What colour is my name?

The journalist Alison Motluk recalls that, when she was writing a short story in high school, her English teacher asked her to change the name of a character. Motluk protested: 'She needs a strong red name.' What did she mean by describing the character's name as 'red'? Well, she meant the same thing I mean when I say a traffic light is red. For Motluk, names have colours, just like physical objects. And not just names: almost all words have colours for her, and even numbers and letters of the alphabet.

This phenomenon is called **synaesthesia**, and it affects about one person in 25,000. People with synaesthesia constantly receive a barrage of sensory impressions denied to the rest of us: they report that white paint smells blue, that grass smells purple, that a hovering helicopter sounds green, that lemons taste pointy while chocolate tastes prickly, that the vowel sound of *coo* appears yellow. One individual has even reported coloured orgasms! Though such people vary in their responses, any one individual is highly consistent: when tested at intervals of many weeks, a synaesthetic almost invariably gives the same responses.

For synaesthetics, spoken language is not just something they hear: they *see* it as a riot of colour. In a recent study in London, blindfolded subjects had their brains monitored by a PET scanner while they listened to spoken words and sounds. The scans showed consistently that, when the synaesthetics heard something, the visual areas of their brains were activated, particularly the areas believed to process colour, while no such activity occurred in the brains of non-synaesthetic control subjects.

Synaesthetic individuals possess their ability from early child-hood, probably from birth, and they are invariably astonished to discover that other people lack the ability. We have almost no idea how synaesthesia works, beyond the obvious conclusion that affected individuals have extra connections in their brains, connections which the rest of us lack. Some investigators have conjectured that all children are born with synaesthesia, but that it disappears in all but a tiny minority of people, and there is a small amount of evidence supporting this idea.

It is easy to get the idea that synaesthetics are supremely fortunate people, living in a rich world to which most of us are blind. Fascinatingly, studies to date have found that synaesthetics are not a random sample of the population: over 50 per cent are left-handed or ambidextrous; all of them have extraordinary memories; most of them are very poor at mathematics and have unusual difficulty in finding their way around; many of them report strange experiences like *déjà vu*, precognitive dreams and clairvoyance. Finally, the overwhelming majority are women. This last finding has revived the old notion, often suggested but so far supported by very little evidence, that men and women have differently structured brains. It is too early to draw any firm conclusions from the existence of synaesthesia. We have seen that there is impressive and growing evidence that our language faculties are largely independent of the other functions of our brains; at the same time, it is becoming ever more apparent that those same language faculties link up with the rest of the brain in complex and wonderful ways.

Further reading

The most readable introduction to psycholinguistics is Aitchison (1989); equally readable, but concerned exclusively with words in the mind, is Aitchison (1987). A good introduction to the organization of the brain is Geschwind (1979). The story of Dr P. is told in the title essay of Sacks (1985). A number of the essays in Pinker (1994) and in Smith (1989) deal with some of the topics discussed in this chapter. There are many university-level textbooks of psycholinguistics; perhaps the most approachable one is Steinberg (1993). Accessible specialist books on slips of the tongue and other speech errors are Fromkin (1973) and Fromkin (1980); see also Motley (1985). A very readable book that places the study of language within the broader study of mind is Gazzaniga (1992). Jackendoff (1993) is a magnificent popular book which attempts to bring together recent work on language, brain, mind and cognition. A popular account of synaesthesia is Motluk (1994).

Chapter 7

Children and language

In contrast with the young of most other mammals (except marsupials), human infants are born at an extraordinarily early stage of development. A baby deer can stand and walk within minutes of birth, but a human infant cannot even turn over or crawl until months after birth. At birth, the infant's skull is not yet fully formed; the myelin sheaths which insulate the neurons in the brain are not yet fully developed; even the visual system in the brain is not yet working properly. Indeed, it has been estimated that human infants really 'ought' not to be born until after eighteen months, instead of the actual nine months.

So why are we born at such an inconveniently early stage of development? There is no simple answer, but one fact stands out: because of their large brains, human infants have extraordinarily large heads, and even at nine months it is barely possible for the infant to squeeze through its mother's birth canal. Presumably another month or so of growth in the womb would render human birth impossible. Even as it is, human birth is conspicuously more difficult, painful and dangerous than birth in other creatures, and it is not at all rare for the infant's brain to be permanently (if harmlessly) deformed by the trauma of birth.

For years after birth, the child remains largely helpless and utterly dependent on its parents for survival. During this time it can hardly do anything for itself at all – except for one thing: it can learn language.

The acquisition of language is arguably the most astonishing and wonderful feat we accomplish in our entire life, and we do it at an age when we can hardly do anything else. Moreover, it is the one thing that children do better than adults: any physically normal child will learn perfectly the language surrounding it, whereas hardly any adults can perform the same feat. How do children do this? How do they acquire their first language?

Until not so many years ago, many people were inclined to try to explain language acquisition in terms of imitation and reinforcement. In this view, the child simply tries to imitate what the grown-ups are saying. If it produces a good imitation, it perhaps gets rewarded with praise and smiles; if it produces a poor imitation, it gets discouraged by frowns or corrections. Consequently, the imitations of adult speech become steadily better, until they are finally indistinguishable from it, and the child has learned the language.

One of the most profound and indisputable achievements of linguistics in recent years has been the demonstration that this 'imitation-and-reinforcement' model is totally, hopelessly, grotesquely wrong. Not only do children not learn language in this way, they couldn't *possibly* learn it in such a way: it would be literally impossible. We now know a good deal about how children actually *do* learn language, and it turns out that the way they do it is far more fascinating than simple-minded imitation hypotheses would suggest.

I'll begin by describing what we can observe by watching a child acquire a first language. From these observations I shall draw some preliminary conclusions. Then I'll look at acquisition in a variety of unusual circumstances, to see how well those preliminary conclusions stand up. Finally, I'll consider the evidence from disability.

What we observe

Language acquisition begins very early, perhaps even before birth. Tests have shown that newborn infants born to French-speaking mothers living in a French-speaking environment much prefer to listen to recordings of French than to recordings of other languages. It must be the intonation and rhythm which attracts them, and we assume that they must have got used to hearing this intonation and rhythm while still in the womb (sound carries through the mother's belly). Already, it appears, the infants are beginning to tune in to the language of their environment and to pay special attention to that language.

After birth, virtually every healthy child goes through the same identifiable stages of acquisition in the same order, though there is considerable variation in the calendar ages at which particular stages are reached.

At around the age of two months, the infant begins **cooing** – making those familiar but hard-to-describe baby noises. Around six months, cooing gives way to **babbling**, a kind of vocal play typically involving strings of syllables. Babbling children often produce sounds which are not present in the surrounding language, as though they were merely experimenting with their vocal tracts, but gradually their babbling becomes more and more attuned to that language. In particular, their babbling starts to show the intonation patterns typical of the surrounding language, and experiments show that at this stage a French-speaking mother can identify French babies (not her own) merely by listening; mothers speaking English, Russian or Arabic can perform the equivalent feat. A very few children fail to babble at all, but no one knows why.

Sometime between ten and twenty months the child finally begins to produce recognizable single words, and we conventionally say at this point that it is beginning to speak. (Curiously, girls tend to start earlier than boys.) This **one-word stage** continues for some time, as the child slowly adds new words to its vocabulary. That vocabulary does not grow rapidly, but it includes several different kinds of words: *daddy*, *doggie*, *spoon*, *bath*, *hot*, *eat*, *up*, *bye-bye*, even *that*. But it does *not* include any grammatical words like *is*, *might*, *of*, *to* or *the*, nor does the child use any grammatical endings such as plurals or past tenses.

Around 18 to 24 months, something momentous happens: the child begins to produce utterances which are two words long: things like *daddy sock*, *want juice* and *gimme spoon*. This **two-word stage** is well named: the child cannot produce any three-word utterances, like *mummy get ball*, but it can say *mummy get* and *get ball*. Importantly, a child at this stage hardly ever says anything like *ball get*, with non-adult word order. Already the child is acquiring some *grammar*: recall from Chapter 2 that word order is an important part of grammar, especially in English. Still, however, there are no grammatical words or endings.

At around the same time, the child's vocabulary begins to grow much more rapidly than before, and parents can no longer keep track of the words their child knows. By the age of five, the average child is thought to know around 10,000 words, which means that it must have been learning them at a rate of about ten a day.

The two-word stage lasts for several months, and then, in the words of the linguist Steven Pinker, 'all hell breaks loose'. Utterances suddenly become much longer: four, five, six, seven, ten words and more. Grammatical words and endings appear and, in a matter of months, the child is using almost the whole range of adult grammatical forms of words. All kinds of new constructions appear – negation, subordinate clauses, questions – and are quickly used with increasing accuracy and confidence.

Here is a sample of utterances from a famous child known in the literature as Adam, studied by the linguist Roger Brown. At 27 months Adam was still producing two-word utterances like *big drum*. By 29 months he was saying *What that paper clip doing?*; by 32 months, *Let me get down with the boots on*; by 36 months, *You dress me up like a baby elephant*; by 38 months, *Can I put my head in the mailbox so the mailman can know where I are and put me in the mailbox?*

And Adam was a *slow* learner. Another child followed in the same study, known as Eve, was producing things like these before she was two: *Fraser, the doll's not in your briefcase* and *I got peanut butter on the paddle*. At the same age, Adam still had some months of two-word utterances ahead of him. Adam and Eve both went through all the same stages, but Eve whizzed through them much faster.

Between the ages of roughly two and three years (earlier for the Eves; later for the Adams), children acquire the vast majority of the grammar of the language they are learning. By age five, they have mastered practically everything, apart from a few elaborate constructions which are not learned until later. They are still making the odd mistake (*two mens*; *I breaked it*), very prominent to adult ears, but studies show that these mistakes are really rather rare: a five-year-old in fact gets pretty much everything right pretty much all of the time. Look at it this way: in spite of making the odd slip, a five-year-old child already knows more about the grammar of English than you can find in any book ever written. Recall what I said in Chapter 2 about the masses of English grammar which you know but probably didn't realize you knew: you had already acquired that knowledge by age five, and most of it by age three.

By any standard, this is a phenomenal achievement: a three-year-old cannot add two numbers, make a phone call, tie her shoelaces or cross the road alone – but she has a magnificent command of the grammar and vocabulary of English, or French, or Basque, or Navaho, or whatever language she is learning. (And children being raised bilingually have that same command of *two* languages!)

After the two-word stage, acquisition proceeds so dizzyingly fast that it is impossible to keep track of everything the child is doing. However, if we focus our attention on one particular aspect of the language at a time, and follow that, we begin to notice some very illuminating data.

A closer look

Consider English plurals. Suppose I tell you (truthfully) that *ziff*, *zo* and *zax* are obscure Scrabble words denoting things that can be counted. What do you suppose their plurals are? No problem for you, I'm sure: *ziffs*, *zos* and *zaxes*. In fact, if you listen carefully, you will notice that the plural ending is pronounced differently in all three cases: the first has an *s*-sound, the second has a *z*-sound, and the third has a *z*-sound preceded by an extra vowel. I'm quite certain you chose the right form of the plural in each case without thinking about it. Included in your knowledge of English grammar is the knowledge of how to make plurals.

Small children can be tested for the same ability, using the **wug test**. A child is shown a cute little figure and told 'Here's a wug.' A second, similar, figure is introduced, and the investigator says 'Look – here's another wug. Now there are two –' A child who says *wugs*, with the ending correctly pronounced like a *z*, has learned to make plurals. Most four-year-olds get this right, and practically everyone gets it right by age six.

Now the child has never heard the made-up word *wug* before, and therefore can never have heard the plural *wugs*. So how does she know that *wugs* is the right plural? It can't possibly be because of imitation or memorization: it can only be because she has constructed a *rule* for making English plurals, a rule which she can apply effortlessly to new nouns, the same rule that you used with my Scrabble words. This is another rule of English grammar, similar to the ones I discussed in Chapter 2, even if it looks a bit simpler than those other rules.

How did she learn that rule? Parents certainly don't drill their children in making plurals: 'Look, Jennifer, one dog, two dogs; one match, two matches.' Even if they did, how would that help? Parents are not aware of the three different forms of the plural ending, and can't point them out. None the less, by the age of four or five, Jennifer has learned the rule. Bear this in mind, if you will, and I'll return to the question a little later.

Now consider how children learn negation. All children do this in exactly the same way. First, they just stick a negative word (usually *no*) at the front of the sentence: *No I want juice*. After a while, that negative word is moved to the front of the verb: *I no want juice*. Finally, the rather complicated English negative auxiliaries appear: *I don't want juice*. And here's the crunch: parents, if they like, can correct the child until they're blue in the face, but she will continue to use her current pattern for making negatives until she's ready for the next stage. Even if they don't correct her (and most parents don't), she will still move through these same stages until she settles on the adult form.

What is she doing? Once again, she is clearly formulating *rules* for making negatives, and she's trying different rules until she finds one that gives her the adult forms. But look: she's not just trying out any old rules. *Every child tries the same rules in the same order.* Moreover, children learning other languages do exactly the same thing – though a child learning, say, Spanish can stop at the second stage, because the *I no want juice* pattern is exactly the way negative sentences are constructed in Spanish.

In other words, *children seem to know what rules they should try!* This is astounding, and it destroys any suggestion of imitation or reinforcement. If the child were really just imitating adult speech, we would expect a more or less random series of approximations to the adult forms, but that is exactly what we don't find. And negatives are in no way exceptional. Precisely the same thing happens with every aspect of language acquisition we look at. Questions, for example, always develop like this: first, *Why you eating?* (no auxiliary); second, *Why you are eating?* (auxiliary not moved); third *Why are you eating?* (auxiliary moved next to question word).

It is time to ponder these observations.

Why is this happening?

We now have an overwhelming mass of observational data demonstrating that children go about the business of language acquisition in a very orderly way. They don't produce random approximations to adult speech, and they don't make random errors, so they can't be working via mere imitation. Any attempts by adults to 'correct' children's utterances have zero effect: the child just works through the various well-ordered stages of acquisition at her own pace, and so reinforcement, positive or negative, cannot be a factor. What the child does is to construct rules of steadily increasing sophistication, and moreover all children seem to try out the same rules in the same order. In other words, language acquisition is an *active* process: the child is not just passively soaking up bits of language which come her way; instead, she is *constructing* the language as she goes. This is one of the central findings of modern linguistics, and it destroys forever any simple-minded notions of imitation or reinforcement.

In fact, a little thought shows that any interpretation of acquisition as a purely passive process is doomed. Consider the famous **gavagai problem**. You are painfully learning a foreign language, when one day a rabbit bounds past. Your teacher looks at it and says 'gavagai'. What does *gavagai* mean? Does it mean 'rabbit'? A particular size or colour of rabbit? Is it the name of that individual rabbit? Does it perhaps mean 'Look at him go', or 'That's good eating', or 'He's ruined my lettuce patch', or any of a trillion other conceivable things? How can you possibly tell?

A child acquiring a first language has the same problem on a colossal scale. How does she know what *anything* means? When she hears an adult utterance, how does she know whether it's intended as the name of some individual entity, as the name of some class of entities, as a comment on some characteristic of some entity, as a description of some activity, or as something else? How can she guess the meaning of something like *Mummy is tired*, or *Daddy's not here*, when she can't even see the tiredness or Daddy?

And it's worse than that. Even if she learns the meanings of some particular utterances, how does she construct generalizations? If she hears an adult say *The dog is hungry* and *My shirt is blue*, how does she know as a result that she can say *Lisa is pretty* or *This glass is dirty*? Yes, of course, all these sentences have similar structures, but how does the child *know* they're similar? If she doesn't have any language to start with, how can she tell that certain words behave like certain other words for the purpose of building sentences?

But children *do* know this. A child hears *Lisa is happy* and *Lisa looks happy*; she then hears *The dog is hungry* and can correctly produce *The dog looks hungry*. But she also hears *Lisa is sleeping* – yet she does *not* produce *Lisa looks sleeping*. No child has ever been heard to make this particular mistake. Why not? Sure, *hungry* is an adjective, while *sleeping* is a verb. But how does the child *know* this? How does she even know that there *are* such things as adjectives and verbs?

This fundamental problem is called the **logical problem of language acquisition**: it seems to be impossible in principle to learn anything about a language without knowing something else about it first. The child can't possibly just memorize all of the infinite number of conceivable utterances along with information about when to use each one (remember my totally new utterances in Chapter 2). And of course she doesn't: she constructs rules instead. But, in order to construct rules, she first has to spot that some utterances are similar to others. But she can't possibly realize that one utterance is similar to another unless she already knows what a similarity looks like. And how does she know that?

Broadly speaking, there have been two kinds of answer offered for this question. Some people have concluded that children acquire language merely by using their ordinary all-purpose cognitive abilities, the same abilities they use to acquire other kinds of knowledge about the world. Others, however, have preferred the answer proposed by the famous American linguist Noam Chomsky. In Chomsky's view, children are *born* knowing what human languages are like – that is, a very considerable part of the structure of human language is innate. Chomsky argues that our species has simply evolved a language faculty which is built into our brains, and that language in large measure just *grows* in children, the way their visual faculties grow. Chomsky's interpretation is still deeply controversial, but there is a growing body of evidence suggesting that he may be right. Let's now look at some of that evidence.

Looking for language

One way of testing Chomsky's hypothesis is to see what children do when they are presented with the problem of learning language in unusual circumstances. Here I shall consider two such circumstances.

First, deaf children. Deaf children coo and babble like other children, but, since they receive no auditory stimuli, their babbling soon dries up and they remain silent. However, if they observe people around them using sign language, they eagerly begin babbling with their hands. If their parents are deaf and hence fluent signers, such children go on to learn sign language normally and perfectly, and they go through all the same stages as speaking children: the one-word and two-word stages, an early absence of grammatical markers followed by increasingly confident mastery of the whole elaborate grammatical apparatus of sign language, and so on. There is absolutely no difference that we can see between the acquisition of spoken language and the acquisition of sign language. Recall from Chapter 6 that even brain damage produces exactly the same consequences in both cases, allowing us to conclude that the language faculty is largely independent of other mental faculties – just as Chomsky's view predicts.

If the deaf child's parents are not completely fluent in sign language, but use it somewhat inconsistently and inaccurately, the child *still* learns the language perfectly. It seems that children are so good at learning language that they can extract the required rules even from poor-quality performances, and hence they learn to use sign language *better than their parents*! (Another nail in the coffin for imitation theories of language-learning.) But now notice something else: if the parents cannot use sign language at all, the deaf child will still seize upon *any* gestures made by the parents and develop those gestures *into its own sign language*! Several such cases have been studied, and there is no doubt of this: such children invent rigid grammatical rules, including things like modification of verbs, and behave just like children learning ordinary sign language, except that they have to invent their own signs. Unfortunately, such home-grown systems only seem to develop to a certain extent, after which further progress is apparently impossible, no doubt due to lack of suitable reinforcement.

What can we make of such observations? There seems only one possible interpretation: as the linguist Ray Jackendoff puts it, children *look for language*. They look first for spoken language; failing that, they look for sign language; failing that, they look for *anything* in the environment which might resemble language, and do their best to turn it into a full-blown language. This is a stunning conclusion, but it can be backed up by further evidence.

Very many times in human history, people from a variety of different places, speaking a variety of different languages, have found themselves brought together in one place. This has happened, for example, to Africans brought as slaves to North America or the

Caribbean; it has happened to the people of Papua New Guinea, united in a new nation speaking hundreds of languages; it has happened to the flood of workers, drawn from a dozen countries, who went to Hawaii to work on the sugar plantations. Having no language in common, such people invariably respond in the same way: they create a **pidgin**. A pidgin is a very basic and crude system of communication, consisting of bits and pieces drawn from several languages and stitched together rather clumsily. A pidgin has no fixed vocabulary and no fixed grammar; indeed, it usually has no recognizable grammar at all. Different individuals speak it differently, and it is a very poor and limited way of communicating, but, for simple purposes, it does work, and pretty much everybody in the community learns to handle it.

After a while, the people using the pidgin get married and have children. These children play with other children in the community, and, whatever they may speak at home, the children have only the pidgin to use with other children. Now here's the big question: what happens?

If you've been following the discussion so far, you can guess: the children take the pidgin and turn it into a real language! Very quickly, they settle on a fixed grammatical system, including, for example, a fixed word order, which pidgins don't have. They introduce all sorts of new grammatical elaborations which are absent from the pidgin: verb tenses, subordinate clauses, everything you'd expect a language to have. They greatly expand the vocabulary until they can talk easily about anything they like. This new language is called a **creole**, and the children who create it are the first native speakers of the creole. In some cases, the creole may survive and flourish. In Haiti, for instance, the first language of the entire population is the creole invented by their mostly African ancestors generations ago, and the very recently invented creole of Papua New Guinea is now widely used there. In other cases, the creole may eventually disappear: for example, Hawaiian Creole has now been almost entirely supplanted by English.

The construction of creoles provides magnificent support for Jackendoff's position, and delivers yet further death blows to those antiquated notions that language acquisition is a passive affair involving imitation and reinforcement. When children invent a creole, not only do they learn a language that their parents don't know, they learn a language that didn't even exist before. It is difficult to conceive of more direct and convincing evidence for the assertion I made earlier in this chapter: children *actively construct their language*.

Is there a cutoff age?

As I've already remarked, children learn perfectly any languages they are exposed to, while most adults can't do this. In the 1960s the neurologist Eric Lenneberg proposed an explanation: children have a distinctive faculty for learning language which is 'switched off' by the body at around age twelve or thirteen. This hypothesis of a **cutoff age** for language acquisition implies that there is a critical period for acquisition, after which it becomes impossible to learn a language. Lenneberg's hypothesis would be easy to test: all we have to do is to raise a child in total isolation from language until the age of fourteen or so and then see if the child can learn a first language. Naturally, no one in his right mind would dream of conducting such a barbarous experiment. Unfortunately, some people are not in their right minds, and the experiment has occasionally been performed. Here I'll consider the cases of three children who were the victims of such an experiment: their real names have been concealed, and they are known in the literature as Isabelle, Genie and Chelsea.

Isabelle, a French girl, was hidden away by her parents for years, and was prevented from hearing any language. Discovered at age six, she had no language and was severely backward in most respects. Placed in a normal environment, however, she began learning French very rapidly, and within one year she was almost indistinguishable from other children of her age. In Lenneberg's view, Isabelle was lucky: she was rescued well before she reached the cutoff age.

Much less fortunate was Genie, whose deranged parents kept her a virtual prisoner throughout her childhood: tied to a potty by day, and into a crib by night, she was never spoken to, she was never allowed to hear speech, and she was punished if she made a sound.

Only at the age of thirteen, on one of her rare trips out of the house with her mother, was she spotted by an alert official and removed from her family.

Placed in more normal surroundings, Genie blossomed. The thin, sad, silent creature turned into a lively and playful girl with a mischievous sense of humour. And almost immediately she started to learn English. She began with one-word utterances, soon progressed to the two-word stage, and rapidly acquired many of the features of English grammar, as well as some hundreds of words. Then, sadly, she stopped. Even after years of intensive coaching, she hardly made any further progress. For example, her use of negation never went beyond the *No I want juice* stage discussed above. Overall, her command of language remained stuck at roughly the stage reached by the average two-and-a-half-year-old, even though in other respects she reached the level of a seven- or eight-year-old.

The tragic case of Genie appears to confirm the hypothesis of a cutoff age, but things are not so simple. When discovered, Genie was severely retarded, and remained so in spite of considerable progress. It is possible that she was retarded at birth, though it seems more likely that she was born normal and that her backwardness was only the result of her long years of barbarous ill-treatment. Still, we cannot entirely rule out the possibility that her failure to learn English was the result merely of her general cognitive disabilities.

The same is not true of Chelsea. Chelsea was born nearly deaf, but, as has happened in hundreds of other such cases, she was disastrously misdiagnosed as mentally retarded when she failed to learn to speak. Unlike the other two children, she was raised by a loving family and allowed to lead as normal a life as possible. Only when she was thirty-one did a disbelieving doctor, seeing her for the first time, spot her deafness and prescribe for her a hearing aid. Able to hear speech at last, she began learning English. After years of intensive training, she had acquired some 2,000 words and the rudiments of English grammar; she could speak, read and understand well enough to lead something approximating to a normal life and even to hold a part-time job. But she never acquired anything approaching a normal command of language, and she too appears to be stuck at roughly the level of a two-and-a-half-year-old.

On balance, then, the evidence presented to us so unkindly by psychopathic parents and bungling doctors appears to confirm Lenneberg's hypothesis: our phenomenal language-learning ability remains with us only for the first few years of life, after which it is shut down by some genetic programming. More and more, it is looking as though language is part of our genetic endowment.

Language in our genes?

Chomsky's innateness hypothesis implies that our language faculty must in large measure reside in our genes. This in turn suggests that genetic defects might have consequences for language acquisition. Of course, no one is suggesting a 'gene for language' – genes don't usually work in such a simple way – but some recent studies have brought unexpected support for a connection between language and genes, and hence for the innateness hypothesis.

There are various types of genetic defects which produce a range of physical and mental abnormalities. It was discovered some years ago that a particular defect on chromosome number eleven induces a disorder of calcium metabolism in our bodies, with highly consistent consequences. Affected children display the **Williams syndrome**: Williams children are small and slight, with several abnormalities of the internal organs and a striking 'pixie-like' face. They are rather severely mentally retarded: even at an advanced age, they cannot add two and two, tie their shoelaces or set a table. They have considerable difficulties with spatial relations. But Williams children can learn language – and how! They learn language in the normal way and quickly become fluent. They speak rapidly and enthusiastically, often in something close to a breathless rush, and indeed researchers have remarked that it is difficult to shut them up. They have large vocabularies, and they can effortlessly construct long and complex sentences: in fact, their grammar is virtually perfect, apart from an occasional tendency to overregularize irregular forms (*taked* for *took*, and so on). They tell elaborate and wonderful stories, though they sometimes have trouble with reality, and may chatter gaily about non-existent friends and happenings. They delight in unusual words. Ask a normal child to name some animals, and you'll get *cat*, *dog*, *cow*, *horse*. Ask a Williams child, and you'll get something like *ibex*, *pteranodon*, *yak*, *unicorn*. On the whole, if you listen to a Williams child, you will hardly notice that anything is wrong – and yet such people must spend their lives in institutions.

What the Williams syndrome shows is that even fairly devastating damage to mental and cognitive processes may leave the language faculty virtually intact. This is striking evidence for the *modularity* hypothesis mentioned in Chapter 6, though on its own it does not prove a connection between language and genes. But now let us consider another disability.

Clinicians have long been aware that certain children who otherwise appear to be normal, healthy and intelligent none the less have great difficulty in learning a first language. Often they start very late, progress slowly, speak slowly and painfully, have trouble completing their sentences, and make lots of mistakes. Some of them, though, speak rapidly and fluently, but with an absolutely horrendous number of grammatical mistakes. Most affected children eventually acquire a more or less adequate command of language, but the disability none the less continues throughout life. This disability is called **Specific Language Impairment**, or **SLI**, a meaningless label which may in fact cover a range of distinct disabilities. Several doctors have noted, however, that SLI tends to run in families – and recently the Canadian-based linguist Myrna Gopnik has discovered, and studied, an entire family in Britain in which no fewer than 16 out of 30 members, spread over three generations, exhibit SLI. Her work has caused a storm of excited discussion.

In this family, SLI is exhibited by the grandmother, by four of her five children, and by eleven of her twenty-four grandchildren, but by none of the offspring of her one unaffected son; males and females are affected equally. One of the affected grandchildren has a twin brother who is unaffected. As usual, all the affected members are otherwise normal, and in particular they all have normal intelligence and normal hearing.

All the afflicted members show the same symptoms. Their speech is slow and laboured, and they stop constantly to correct themselves, but as often as not they 'correct' proper forms to improper ones. Their spontaneous speech is full of grammatical errors

– not in overall sentence structure, but in word forms. They regularly leave off grammatical word-endings or use the wrong ones, producing things like *There's a trains coming* or *Yesterday I eat dinner late*. These are mistakes which normal school-age children *never* make – yet these are adults between 40 and 76 years old, and children between eight and nineteen years, at the time of the study. Moreover, all but the grandmother have received intensive therapy intended to correct their problems – obviously, to no great effect.

When Gopnik tested the afflicted family members, she found that they were virtually incapable of distinguishing correct and incorrect grammatical forms or of choosing correct ones. Asked whether *The boy eat three cookie* is right or wrong, they have no idea. Asked to complete *Every day he walks three miles. Yesterday he . . .*, they respond with *walk*. Most strikingly, they fail the *wug test* discussed above. Asked to pluralize *wug*, they produce *wugss* or *wugness*; for the plural of *zat* they give *zackle* or *zacko*; for *zoop* they give *zoopez*, for *zash*, *zatches*; for *tob*, *tobyes*. What on earth is going on here?

Gopnik offers two conclusions. (1) These people have never grasped that there are *rules* for making things like plurals and past tenses. Instead, they simply have to learn every single plural and past-tense form separately, just the way we all do with irregular ones like *men* and *took*, and hence they have no idea what the plural of a new word might be. (2) The distribution of the disability in the family is *exactly* what we would expect to see if the problem were caused by a defective gene which is dominant – that is, if you only need one faulty gene to inherit the problem. Hence these people have inherited a genetic defect.

Since this defective gene has no known consequences apart from an inability to construct certain types of grammatical rule, it may be that we have here direct evidence that our language faculty is genetically controlled. Of course, the particular faulty gene involved has not so far been identified, and it remains a conjecture, though a highly plausible one. The popular press has seized upon Gopnik's 'grammar gene' with delight, but unfortunately many of the journalists who have written about it have completely misunderstood the meaning of the term *grammar*, and have reached the preposterous conclusion that speakers of non-standard English who say *I ain't got none* have a genetic problem (on this, see Chapter 8).

Chomsky's innateness hypothesis remains a matter of controversy, but there is an impressive and growing body of evidence that he is right: that our unique and astounding faculty of language, which is not shared by any other creatures, has come about because some of our remote ancestors evolved it. Like the wings and the navigational systems of birds, like the bee dance, like the echo-locating sonar of bats, our language faculty, we now strongly suspect, is built into our genes.

Further reading

There are many good introductions to child language. Peccei (1994) is brief and elementary; Aitchison (1989) is more detailed but very readable; Elliot (1981) is a university-level text. The children Adam and Eve are described in Brown (1973). Jackendoff (1993) and Pinker (1994) are both wonderful books which embed the study of child language into larger issues; both books provide much more detailed discussion of the issues presented in this chapter. Many of the essays in Ingram (1992) centre on topics from this chapter; though a popular survey, this book is well written. The evidence from creoles is evaluated in Bickerton (1981), but be aware that Bickerton's bold interpretations are still somewhat controversial, while the more dramatic conclusions in his recent (1990) book are *very* controversial. The story of Genie is told in Curtiss (1977) and reviewed in Rymer (1993).

Chapter 8

Attitudes to language

In one of the lesser-known skits performed by the immortal comedy team Monty Python, an interviewer is talking to the Oxford Professor of Medieval History about the medieval open-field farming system. As the two of them drone on about the rights and obligations of freemen and villeins, the audience are giggling uncontrollably. Why? Because, although the interviewer sounds like any other interviewer, the 'Oxford Professor' speaks throughout the discussion in a broad Cockney accent – that is, in the working-class accent of London. In Britain, an Oxford professor just *does not* speak with that sort of accent. Consequently, even though what the 'Professor' says is perfectly sensible and informative, it sounds hilarious to British ears: British listeners find it impossible to take seriously a professor with a working-class urban accent who expresses agreement with *'s right, yeah* instead of with *yes, indeed*.

We have already seen that language is exceptional in a number of respects, both on the planet as a whole and among human attributes. It is also, however, very unusual in the way people react to it. In this chapter we shall be looking at some typical, yet striking, examples of people's attitudes to language.

Can language be immoral?

The ancient Greek philosopher and scientist Aristotle made important contributions to a number of disciplines (including linguistics, but that is not our concern here). Such was Aristotle's pre-eminence that, throughout the Middle Ages in Europe, his every pronouncement was accepted without question. Some of his most impressive work was done in biology, where he proved to be a sharp-eyed observer. However, in one of his books, he makes the following assertion: women have fewer teeth than men.

Now, while I admit I have not made a careful study, I am supremely confident that, if you examine the teeth of the people in your part of the world, you will find that the women have exactly the same number of teeth as the men: thirty-two. What should we make of this conflict between Aristotle's description and our observations? Well, there are two possible responses:

1   The description is wrong: Aristotle's account is at least inadequate and possibly seriously in error.
2   The facts are wrong: women are not growing their teeth right, and we should take steps to make them grow their teeth properly.

How do you react to these two conclusions? Well, unless you are a *very* unusual person, you doubtless find position 1 to be the only possible response, while position 2 is merely insane.

Let's try a similar question from a very different domain. The distinguished American historian Crane Brinton once published a study of revolutions, in which he concluded that every revolution always proceeds in the same way, with the same stages occurring in the same order. Now consider the Nicaraguan revolution of 1979. Suppose, for the sake of argument, that we examined the Nicaraguan revolution and found that it did not proceed at all according to

Professor Brinton's description: suppose that different things happened in a different order. Now, if you discovered this, what would be your response?

1   The description is wrong: Professor Brinton's account is at least inadequate and possibly seriously in error.
2   The facts are wrong: the Nicaraguans didn't do their revolution right, and we should declare it invalid and make them do it over again properly.

How do you react this time? Once again, I am confident, you find position 1 to be the only possibility, while position 2 could only be taken seriously by a candidate for the funny farm.

Why am I asking these dumb questions? Well, let's look at just one more. There is a construction in English which is traditionally known as the *split infinitive*. The 'split infinitive' (this traditional name is in fact grossly misleading) is illustrated by examples like *I want to gradually save enough money to buy a car* and *She decided to never touch another cigarette*, in which the sequences *to gradually save* and *to never touch* are the 'split infinitives'. Now, for over 200 years, grammarians and English teachers have roundly condemned the split infinitive, declaring it to be 'ungrammatical' and 'not English'. None the less, even the most casual observation of English speech reveals that virtually all speakers of English use this construction spontaneously and frequently: it is a prominent feature of spoken English all over the world. Again, the description and the facts are clearly in conflict. What is your response?

1   The description is wrong: the grammarians' account is at least inadequate and possibly seriously in error.
2   The facts are wrong: English-speakers are not speaking their language right, and we should take steps to make them speak it properly.

And how do you feel this time? Well, I can't speak for you, but I can tell you that very large numbers of well-educated English-speakers have this time opted for position 2: they agree that it is the facts that are wrong, and they try desperately to avoid uttering any split infinitives, producing as a result things like *I want gradually to save enough money to buy a car.*

Now, on the face of it, this reaction is simply astounding. People who accept the second position are clearly agreeing that the grammarians' description must be right merely because it has been asserted by prominent authorities and appears in all the books, and they are further agreeing that the facts should therefore be changed to match the description.

How can this be so? If your mechanic tells you your car's fan belt is fine when you can see for yourself that it's broken, you find a new mechanic. If a shop assistant assures you that a purple and orange microskirt and a fishnet top are just the thing to wear to a job interview with a bank, you try another shop. If a real-estate agent tells you that a house perched on the edge of a crumbling cliff is a good buy, when you can see that the house next door has just fallen over the edge, you find a new estate agent. In almost every area of human activity, if even the most distinguished expert tries to tell you something which is blatantly not true, you ignore it and find somebody more sensible to talk to.

But language appears to be an exception. When it comes to language, the response which, almost everywhere else, is transparently insane suddenly seems to many people to be reasonable, to be sensible, to be the only possible response: such people are quite happy to agree that, this time, it is the facts which are wrong and the facts which must be changed. This curious but very widespread view is called **prescriptivism**. Prescriptivism is the belief that we have no business speaking our language in the way that seems natural to us, but that instead we should deliberately change our language to make it conform to the regulations laid down by some group of self-appointed experts – no matter how ignorant or crazy those regulations might appear.

Prescriptivists do not confine their attacks to the 'split infinitive'. Prescriptive grammarians have also declared that it is ungrammatical to say *It's me*, and that the only acceptable form is *It's I*. But *everybody* says *It's me.* Can you imagine looking at a bad photograph of yourself and exclaiming *Good heavens! Is that really I?* The form *It's me* has been universal in English for centuries, whereas *It's I* is little more than a bizarre invention of the prescriptivists, cobbled together out of some confused notion of logic: we are told by the prescriptivists that *It's I* is somehow more 'logical' than *It's me*, whatever that means, and hence that there is something disgraceful about using our native English form. Most people, fortunately, pay no attention to this nonsense, but a nervous minority have allowed themselves to be so browbeaten by the 'experts' that they self-consciously trot out comical locutions like *The person you're looking for is I*. Not long ago, a well-known newspaper columnist who writes on English usage got so carried away with the ridiculous campaign against *It's me* that he condemned the ancient phrase *Woe is me* and urged his readers to 'correct' this 'barbarism' to *Woe is I* – only to beat a shamefaced retreat a week or two later, after a horde of his better-informed readers had pointed out to him that *Woe is me* has been in the language for over a thousand years and literally means 'Woe is to me' (compare the equivalent German *Weh ist mir*). But then prescriptivism does not attach much importance to facts: it deals in personal tastes and prejudices and in declarations handed down from on high.

Prescriptivists also condemn perfectly normal utterances like *Who did you see?*, demanding instead that we should all say *Whom did you see?*, on the preposterous ground that this is what people said five hundred years ago. Well, so they did, but can you see any sense in artificially resuscitating this one particular dead form from among the thousands that litter the history of our language, merely because some little group of fanatics has taken a liking to it? Five hundred years ago people were also saying *He is yclept John* instead of *He is called John*: why not revive this form as well? This would be every bit as sensible as reviving that defunct *whom*.

Another pet dislike of the prescriptive grammarians is the familiar English practice of ending a sentence with a preposition: instead of the perfectly normal *Who are you staying with?*, the prescriptivists tell us, we should say *With whom are you staying?* Why? No reason. The prescriptivists just don't like prepositions at the ends of sentences, that's all, even though they are so much a part of English grammar that we would find it virtually impossible to do without them. The little boy, in bed upstairs, who complained to his father *Daddy, what did you bring that book I didn't want to be read to out of up for?* was speaking normal, grammatical English, and I defy anyone to rearrange this into a form with no prepositions at the end. Winston Churchill, who was not intimidated by such declarations, once wittily replied to someone who had criticized his final prepositions 'This is an outrage up with which I shall not put.'

Such examples could be multiplied at tedious length. Generations of English-speakers have allowed themselves to be browbeaten into believing that there must be something wrong with their language, since it doesn't seem to match up with what the books say English is like. But why? Well, I think that the use of language has somehow come to be viewed by many people as a matter of morality.

It is clear that the declarations in favour of *It's I* and against split infinitives and sentence-final prepositions are in no way descriptions of English. Instead, they are merely somebody's opinion about what English-speakers *ought* to do, much like the opinions about what car drivers ought to do which I mentioned in Chapter 2. Now opinions can be good opinions, but there are also bad opinions, and I would suggest that all four of the ones which I have cited here are very bad opinions indeed. They derive, not from observation, nor even from an admirable desire to improve clarity or grace. Instead, they derive from nothing more than prejudice, confusion and ignorance. We would all be better off if these ridiculous and wrong-headed notions could be dumped on the scrap heap and forgotten. But this is not likely to happen, because, ignorant as they are, these opinions have, for some people at least, acquired the status of moral imperatives. However independent-minded we may be when it comes to ridiculous opinions about teeth or clothes or dodgy houses, we are often, in matters of language, every bit as eager to accept preposterous opinions as the emperor who was told how wonderful his new clothes were. Many of us appear to believe that ignoring or rejecting received opinions about language, no matter how silly those opinions are, is in some mysterious way immoral.

And that, I am convinced, is the driving force behind the campaign for *whom*. Some people have decided that saying *Whom did you see?* is a moral responsibility, part of the definition of a decent, upright person, while *Who did you see?* is a serious moral lapse, on a par with patronizing dirty bookshops and cheating on your income tax. This may seem a surprising conclusion, but I can see no other explanation.

What's happening to our language?

We saw in Chapter 5 that change is a constant and unavoidable feature of every language. During any person's lifetime, the language acquires a number of new words, meanings, pronunciations and grammatical forms, and at the same time loses a number of old ones. And not everybody is happy about this. Take a look at a few English sentences:

(8.1) Fortunately, I have a spare fan belt.
(8.2) Frankly, you ought to stop seeing Bill.
(8.3) Mercifully, the ceasefire appears to be holding.
(8.4) Undoubtedly, she has something up her sleeve.
(8.5) Hopefully, we'll be there in time for lunch.
(8.6) Honestly, you have no taste in clothes.

Does anything strike you as odd about these sentences? Or do they all seem perfectly normal? Well, for most people they *are* perfectly normal. In fact, I'll go further: five of them are probably perfectly normal for everybody. But one of them is different.

The one that causes trouble for some people is number (8.5). A small minority of English-speakers not only reject examples like (8.5) but do so with steam coming out of their ears. The problem for such speakers is the way the word *hopefully* is used here. And they don't just dislike this use of *hopefully*: they're *infuriated* by it. Here is what Mr Philip Howard, a well-known writer on language, has to say about it: he describes this use of *hopefully* as 'objectionable', 'ambiguous', 'obscure', 'ugly', 'aberrant', 'pretentious' and 'illiterate'; finally, playing his ace, he asserts that it was 'introduced by sloppy American academics'. In short, he dislikes it quite a lot.

Philip Howard is not alone in his dislike of this usage: many other writers have complained about it, often with similar bitterness. But why should a usage which seems so natural and unremarkable to most of the population attract such hostility from the rest?

163

All of the words set off by commas in my examples are instances of what linguists call **sentence adverbs**, but the key point is that, while the others have been in the language for several generations at least, *hopefully* only began to be widely used as a sentence adverb two or three decades ago. That is, this particular one happens to be a fairly recent innovation, just one more recent change in the long history of change in English.

Now the people who object to this use of *hopefully* are, almost without exception, middle-aged or older. That is, they are people who had already been using English for several decades before this particular innovation became prominent. Moreover, they are mostly also people who are especially well educated, and who take a particular interest in the use of language. Such people are often very conservative in their view of language; they are perhaps particularly inclined to view any changes in the English they grew up with as instances of 'sloppiness' or 'corruption'. Younger speakers, in contrast, have grown up with this new usage, and they regard it as perfectly normal.

There is nothing novel about the furore over *hopefully*. Similar fulminations can be found at every point in the history of English, or of any other language for which we have records. How do you feel about the following examples?

(8.7) My car is being repaired.

(8.8) My house is being painted.

(8.9) This problem is being discussed at today's meeting.

Anything strange here? I doubt it – I don't think there's an English-speaker alive who regards these as other than normal.

But it wasn't always so. Until well into the eighteenth century, this particular construction did not exist in standard English, and an English-speaker would have had to say *My car is repairing*, *My house is painting* and *This problem is discussing at today's meeting* – forms which are absolutely impossible for us now. But these *were* the normal forms in the eighteenth century, and, when some innovating speakers of English began to say things like *My house is being painted*, the linguistic conservatives of the day could not contain their fury. Veins bulging purply from their foreheads, they attacked the new construction as 'clumsy', 'illogical', 'confusing' and 'monstrous'. But their efforts were in vain. Today all those who objected to the innovation are long dead, and the traditional form which they defended with such passion is dead with them. The 'illogical' and 'monstrous' new form has become the only possibility, and even the most careful and elegant writer of English would not dream of trying to get away with the defunct older form. And you are probably marvelling at this eighteenth-century fury and wondering what all the fuss was about, just as the next generation will read in puzzlement about the attacks on *hopefully* and wonder what all the fuss was about.

Two thousand years ago Roman writers were making similarly hostile comments about the changes which were occurring in the spoken Latin of their day. Their dismay at the increasing 'corruption' of the language had, of course, no effect at all, and the increasingly 'corrupt' spoken Latin continued to change ('deteriorate') until it had developed into such modern languages as Spanish, French and Italian. Naturally, the speakers of these languages do not regard them as corrupt, but as rich, beautiful and expressive. More precisely, the linguistic conservatives in Spain, France and Italy have great admiration for the language they grew up with, but they have some very harsh words for some of the things the young people seem to be saying these days. At every time, and in every place, there is a body of conservative opinion which holds that the language reached some kind of pinnacle of perfection a generation or so ago, and is now going rapidly downhill with all these 'ugly', 'sloppy', 'illiterate' new usages we keep hearing nowadays.

Linguistic purism

There is one particular type of change that often attracts particular condemnation, sometimes even decades or centuries after it has occurred. This is borrowing. As we saw in Chapter 5, very few languages are spoken in total isolation: the speakers of most languages are in contact with speakers of other languages, and one of the most obvious results of such contact is that words are borrowed from one language to another. Again, not everyone is happy about this. Linguistic conservatives sometimes object to the presence in their language of large numbers of loan words, which they regard as a kind of 'contamination' sullying the 'purity' of their language; they may therefore agitate for 'purification' of the language by replacing foreign loans with 'genuine' native words.

Though English is second to none in its appetite for borrowing foreign words, in the last few decades English has been primarily a donor language. English is the world's premier language for science, for technology, for business, and for popular culture, and English words have accordingly flooded into French, Spanish, German, Italian, and even Japanese in vast numbers. Open any popular European or Japanese magazine, and you will see the pages spattered with English loans. I've just picked up an Italian magazine at random; on almost every page someone is described as a *rockstar*, a *top model*, a *sex-symbol* or a *top manager*. An advertisement for a computer promises a *hard disk*, a *mouse* and a *floppy*. One film is labelled a *horror*, while another has a *happy-end*. Fashion articles talk about the *look* and explain what's currently *in*. And the pages are thick with English words like *jogging*, *fan*, *gadget*, *hobby*, *T-shirt*, *massage parlour*, *zoom*, *pay-tv*, *show*, *home video*, *mass media*, *status* and *checkup*.

This fondness for English loans has particularly upset the linguistic conservatives in France. Before the rise of English earlier in this century, French was the world's most prestigious language, and the French have not found it easy to accept the present dominance of English. Appalled by the hundreds of English words pouring into French every year, the French authorities have made determined and even desperate efforts to curb this trend by thinking up 'genuine' French replacements and demanding that French citizens should use only these 'genuine' French words. Thus, while the Germans, the Italians and the Japanese are happy to buy a *computer* with *software*, a *light pen* and a *floppy*, the French are obliged to buy an *ordinateur* with *logiciel*, a *crayon optique* and a *disquette*. The English word *debug* (as in *to debug a program*) was at first borrowed directly as the awkward *débugger*, but the authorities have now decreed that the word should be *déboguer*, which at least looks more French. This last example is reminiscent of an earlier attempt at replacing the English loan *bulldozer* with the 'genuine' French creation *bouledozeur*!

To be fair, the French linguistic authorities have had some success in keeping at least some of the more blatant English loan words out of the language, but nevertheless French-speakers still spend *le weekend* indulging in *le camping*; they listen to *un CD* or *un Walkman*, and they may have a taste for *le rock* or *le jazz* or *le blues* or even *le heavy metal*. If they fancy an evening out, they may go to *le pub* to have *un scotch* or *un gin* or *un cocktail*, or go to see *un western* or *un strip-tease*; if not, they may stay home to read *un best-seller* or just to watch *le football* on television. (And, to my considerable astonishment, the French authorities, worried by the spread of AIDS, have just launched a billboard campaign for condoms featuring a pretty young woman sticking her tongue out, with the caption *Préservatifs: Fuck Aids*. Apparently vernacular English is now thought to have a place in French, at least when it is a matter of some urgency to communicate with young people.) This hostility to loan words from other languages is called **purism**, and it is a widespread phenomenon.

One way of practising purism is to favour the adoption of calques. A **calque** (or **loan-translation**) is a very subtle way of borrowing a foreign word. Instead of taking over the foreign word bodily, the borrowing language instead translates it literally, piece by piece, thereby obtaining something that at least looks like a native word.

The ancient Romans often used this technique for deriving words from the then more prestigious Greek. For example, the Greek word *sympathia* consists of two pieces: a prefix *syn-*, meaning 'with', and a stem *pathia*, meaning 'suffering'. The Romans translated this by using their own prefix *con-* 'with' and the Latin stem *passio* 'suffering', obtaining the Latin calque *compassio*. The speakers of German then in turn calqued the Latin word with the German elements *mit* 'with' and *Leid* 'suffering', producing *Mitleid*, which is the German word for 'sympathy' or 'compassion'. In the same way, the Latin word *expressio*, formed from *ex* 'out' and *pressio* 'pressing', was calqued into German as *Ausdruck*, from *aus* 'out' and *Druck* 'pressure'.

Latin and German are two languages which have relied heavily upon calquing as an alternative to straight borrowing, but perhaps the European champion in this regard is Hungarian. The Greek words *thermos* 'heat' and *metron* 'measure' are the source of the word which appears in English as *thermometer*, in French as *thermomètre*, in Spanish as *termómetro*, in German as *Thermometer*, in Welsh as *thermomedr*, in Basque as *termometro*, in Turkish as *termometre*, in Russian as *termometr*, in Swedish as *termometer*, and so on all across Europe – except in Hungarian, in which the word is *hőmérő*, a calque constructed from the Hungarian words for 'heat' and 'measure'.

English, of course, has always preferred borrowing to calquing, and we have happily borrowed the Latin words *expression* and *compassion*, and the Greek word *sympathy* as well, for good measure. This massive borrowing has rarely bothered anyone, but the nineteenth-century Dorset poet William Barnes did raise a lonely protest, suggesting, for example, that the word *omnibus* (modern *bus*) should be replaced by *folkwain* (a word which is curiously identical in formation to the name of the German car *Volkswagen*). Few have ever listened to such pleas, but, in 1966, the humorist Paul Jennings did offer, in the pages of *Punch* magazine, a sample of what English might have been like if we had followed the example of the Hungarians. Here is an extract, in which the author adopts the conceit that William of Normandy was defeated at Hastings:

> In a foregoing piece (a week ago in this same mirthboke) I wrote anent the ninehundredth yearday of the Clash of Hastings; of how in that mighty tussle, which othered our lore for coming hundredyears, indeed for all following aftertide till Domesday, the would-be ingangers from France were smitten hip and thigh; and of how, not least, our tongue remained selfthrough and strong, unbecluttered and unbedizened with outlandish Latin-born roots of French outshoot.... Our Anglish tongue, grown from many birth-ages of yeomen, working in field or threshing-floor, ringing-loft or shearing house, mead and thicket and ditch, under the thousand hues and scudding clouds of our ever-othering weather, has been enmulched over the hundredyears with many sayings born from everyday life.

It has an unbettered muchness of samenoiselike and again-clanger wordgroups, such as *wind and water*, *horse and hound*, *block and tackle*, *sweet seventeen*, ... The craft and insight of our Anglish tongue for the more cunning switchmeangroups, for unthingsome and overthingsome withtakings, gives a matchless tool to bards, deepthinkers and trypiecemen.

A few of Jennings's coinages may be difficult: *samenoiselike* means 'onomatopoeic', *againclanger* means 'alliterative', *switchmeangroup* means 'metaphor', *unthingsome* means 'abstract', *overthingsome* means 'metaphysical', *withtaking* means 'concept' (this is a calque), and *trypiece* means 'essay'.

How does this strike you? Would English be better off without its tens of thousands of loan words? Would the language be richer and more expressive if we said *foregoing* instead of 'preceding', *yearday* instead of 'anniversary', *othering* instead of 'changing', *hundredyear* instead of 'century', *inganger* instead of 'invader', *outshoot* instead of 'derivation', *enmulch* instead of 'enrich', *unbettered* instead of 'unsurpassed', *deepthinker* instead of 'philosopher'? Well, this is an academic question if ever there was one: there is surely no possibility that we will ever try to ape the French and purge our language of all those loan words.

Finally, before leaving Jennings, I might point out that he has slipped up slightly: the words *noise*, *age* and *piece*, which appear in the passage, are in fact loans from French, if perhaps rather well-disguised ones, while *bard* is a loan from Irish or Welsh. Even with scrupulous attention, it is not easy to get through an English sentence without using any loan words. In any case, few have thought it worth the effort: linguistic purism does not appear to be a force among speakers of English.

On talking proper

In the region of western New York State in which I was brought up, as indeed in a huge part of the English-speaking regions of the world, the form *doesn't* scarcely exists in vernacular speech. Where I come from, almost everyone says *It don't matter* and *He don't need that* –

and these forms are surely very familiar to you as well, no matter where you come from.

Naturally, my high-school English teacher, Mrs Breck, took strong exception to this usage, and she relentlessly waged her own little war upon it. I well remember sitting in class one day when her campaign was in full swing. Having heard my classmate Norman say, for the seven hundredth time that day, something like 'He don't know that', she decided to strike: 'He *doesn't* know that, Norman.' Yeah, that's right', replied Norman, 'he don't.' 'Not *don't*, Norman', reiterated Mrs Breck, her face turning an interesting colour, 'say "he DOESN'T know that".' 'But ... but ...' A look of perplexity suffused Norman's face. 'But it don't *sound* right!'

This little episode encapsulates very neatly the contrast between the very special position of one particular form of English, which we call **standard English**, and all the other varieties of English that there are, which we may collectively term **non-standard English**. The job of an English teacher is very largely to inculcate standard English into her charges, who in most cases do not come already equipped with it. The great majority of English-speakers grow up learning and speaking the local vernacular form of English, which is almost always significantly different from standard English, and is sometimes spectacularly different. Why should this be so?

For many people, the answer is blindingly obvious: 'English is standard English by definition. Standard English is grammatical, logical and expressive; non-standard English is ungrammatical, illogical and ugly, and it just doesn't obey the rules. People who speak non-standard English do so because they are too lazy, too ignorant or too slovenly to learn to speak correctly.'

Not to put too fine a point on it, this opinion is so much hogwash. (I would have used a stronger word, but I'm afraid this chapter has already made my editor nervous.) It does not remotely approximate to the truth.

Speakers of standard English are in fact a minority. Most English-speakers regularly use such widespread forms as *I ain't got none* or *I seen him yesterday, but I ain't seen him today* or *Me and him was there*; depending on where they live, they will also use such localized forms as *Ye divvent knaa, div ye?* in northeastern England

(= 'You don't know, do you?') or *I done shot me a squirrel* in the southern USA (= 'I shot a squirrel'). Such forms may indeed sound bewildering, or even shocking, to speakers of standard English, but is there any reason to declare them 'ungrammatical' or 'illogical'?

Certainly not. Consider my classmate Norman again. Norman said (and probably still says today) *he don't* because that's the form that everybody uses back home, and that's the form he heard and learned when he was growing up. And his reaction to Mrs Breck's suggested *he doesn't* is most instructive: he rejected it because, in his variety of English, *it was ungrammatical*. From his point of view, *he doesn't* was just as strange and ungrammatical as the *he divvent* of Newcastle. Norman was not lazy, or ignorant, or slovenly: he had learned the local variety of English perfectly well, and, like any native speaker of any language, he knew perfectly well what the rules of his English permitted, and he knew what was or was not grammatical. Norman's English had just as many grammatical rules as any other variety of English. It's merely that the variety of English he had learned did not enjoy the privileged position of being the standard variety.

Nor is it possible to maintain that *he don't* is somehow 'less logical' than *he doesn't*. Certainly *he don't* is no more illogical than the irregular *he won't*, but *he won't* happens to be standard English, and no speaker of standard English is prepared to condemn *he won't* merely because it is 'illogical', or to insist on a 'more logical' form like *he willn't*. Purely as a result of historical accident, *he won't* happens to have been selected, from among several competitors, as the standard form, while *he don't*, also with several competitors, happens not to have been so fortunate as to be selected. This is perhaps slightly surprising, since the number of English-speakers who say *he don't* is almost certainly greater than the number who say *he doesn't*.

In fact, it makes absolutely no sense to describe a verb form as 'logical' or 'illogical'. An argument may be logical or not; the structure of an essay may perhaps be logical or not. But it makes no more sense to say that *doesn't* is a 'logical' verb form than it does to assert that *cat* is the 'logical' word for a feline, or to claim that using *you* to address either one person or a hundred people is 'logical'. Standard English has no particular logic on its side.

What then *does* it have on its side? Nothing more than prestige, deriving from an agreement among educated speakers that certain forms should be accepted as standard, while other forms should not. How did this agreement come about?

When the Anglo-Saxons settled England some 1,500 years ago, they were already speaking English in a number of rather divergent regional varieties. Our earliest Old English texts already show this variation quite graphically. As time passed, the ordinary processes of linguistic change, as always, produced increasing regional fragmentation. These processes have continued down to the present day, with the result that we see great differences in the English spoken in different places. Such differences are evident in every aspect of the language; here we shall consider only verb forms.

Consider the verb *be*. In very early Old English, the forms of this verb became hopelessly entangled with the forms of two other verbs of similar meaning, producing, in standard English, the startlingly irregular forms *I am, you are, he is, I was, you were, I have been*, and so on. Every local variety of English has sorted out the resulting mess in its own way, which is nearly always different from the standard arrangement. Thus, for example, in the English county of Somerset, the forms which people settled on were as follows: *I be, thou art, he be, we be, you be, they be*. In much of the north of England, however, the form *is* was generalized, producing *I is, you is, he is, we is, you is, they is*. Some western varieties generalized *am* instead, producing *I am, you am, he am, we am, you am, they am*. Other regions settled on different patterns, so that all of *I am, I is, I are, I be* and *I bin* are well attested in England. Much the same is true in the past tense: some varieties have generalized *was* (*I was, you was, we was, ...*), while others have generalized *were* (*I were, you were, he were, ...*). Now none of the attested patterns has any claim to greater logic than any other; some are more regular than others, that's all, and the set of forms which has become standard is one of the craziest of the lot.

Such forms as *I seen her, I done it, I drawed a picture, I writ a letter, I've took a picture*, and others too numerous to list, are all exceedingly common in English, but these forms have not had the good fortune to be accepted into the standard variety of English.

Even standard English is not quite entirely uniform. American English has *I got a letter yesterday*, but *I've just gotten a letter*; in England, where the same forms were formerly considered standard, the second has been replaced by a new standard form, *I've just got a letter* (= 'I've just received a letter'). On the other hand, standard British agrees with standard American in having *I've forgotten her name*; the form *I've forgot her name*, while widespread, is not at present admitted as standard – but it might be, one of these days.

How did the choices get made? Who or what determined which forms would become standard and which should be relegated to the outer darkness of non-standard status? Mostly, it was an accident. By the early modern period (the fifteenth and sixteenth centuries), regional differences among English-speakers had become so great that people from different parts of England were often finding it genuinely difficult to understand one another. Since this was a time of increasing travel, increasing trade and increasing literacy, some kind of solution had to be found. Unlike the French (and others), the English never saw fit to establish a language academy to hand down rulings from on high. Instead, the problem was solved by political factors. The capital city of London, and the region around it, had become by far the most important region of the country – politically (the court was there, and it was the hub of the legal and administrative systems), economically (it was the centre of commerce and banking), and culturally (the great universities of Oxford and Cambridge were nearby).

This was enough to settle matters. The particular varieties of English used in and around London came increasingly to be regarded as the most prestigious and desirable type of English. Ambitious men and women from the provinces came to the London area to make their fortunes, and they adjusted their speech to the forms they heard there. As a consequence, the particular words and forms that were typical of the Home Counties (as the area around London is known) gradually came to be regarded as the standard version of English, even if they were hardly used anywhere else, while forms not used in the Home Counties, however widespread they might be in the country as a whole, did not achieve standard status. Hence the particular verb forms that we now regard as standard are, for the most part, no more than those forms that happened to be in use in the London area.

It is important to realize that the forms of standard English are largely the result of a historical accident. If some other region of England had happened to achieve political pre-eminence, then forms like *he don't* and *they was* might now be regarded as standard, and ferocious English teachers would now be doing their best to stamp out such 'ignorant' and 'illiterate' usages as *he doesn't* and *they were*.

Even standard forms are not totally resistant to change. Several centuries ago, the standard English form was *I catched a cold*, but the 'ignorant' new form *caught* (apparently modelled on *taught*) has now replaced the earlier *catched*, and now it is *catched* which is regarded as 'ignorant'. In American English, *I dived into the water* has recently been replaced, for a majority of speakers (including me), by *I dove into the water*, making this verb work just like *drive/drove*.

Be that as it may, we now have, by whatever series of accidents, a generally agreed standard version of English. How should we regard it? Well, above all, standard English is a *convenience*. Speakers from Glasgow, Newcastle, New Orleans and Cape Town are likely to have considerable trouble in understanding one another if they all insist on using their own local varieties of English. The existence of an agreed standard form, learned by all educated English-speakers everywhere, makes it much easier for all these people to talk to one another.

No particular variety of English is intrinsically better or worse than other varieties. Just about any variety of English would have made a satisfactory standard, if it had happened to be selected. As it happens, one particular variety of English has been selected, as a result of a series of historical accidents, to be our standard, and that variety is, of course, perfectly satisfactory for the purpose. Just like a standard electrical plug, a standard form of English is an enormous convenience for all speakers of the language. Regardless of how I speak when I'm talking to my mother or my sister, when I write this book, I write it in standard English, the same standard English that you've learned, no matter where you grew up, and hence you can read what I write without difficulty.

In fact, in the complex world we live in today, standard English has become more than a mere convenience: it is now a necessity. No

English-speaker can hope to prosper in the wider world without an adequate command of the standard dialect (for that is what standard English is: one dialect among many). We simply have too many dealings with too many other English-speakers from all over the world to be able to get by only with the local variety we grew up with, and a speaker who cannot function effectively in standard English is at a very serious disadvantage. Sadly, many such people exist, and most of them are condemned to low-paid dead-end jobs with no prospects, or even to long-term unemployment. My old high-school English teacher may not have understood why Norman spoke the way he did, but she knew that his non-standard speech was not going to help him to get ahead.

This state of affairs is well understood in some other parts of the world. Consider Germany. The regional dialects of German differ so greatly that speakers from, say, Berlin and Bonn cannot understand each other at all if they use their local vernaculars. Consequently, German-speakers use their local variety when talking to others from their area and standard German when talking to everybody else: that is, German-speakers are typically **bidialectal**. Almost no one in Germany regards the numerous non-standard local varieties as ignorant or slovenly or illiterate: these varieties are merely seen as having a different function from the standard.

In the English-speaking countries, however, the attitude is very different. Non-standard regional varieties of English are, as we have already seen, constantly condemned in the most offensive terms. This attitude is ignorant and shameful. It is one thing to try to give everyone an adequate command of standard English for those occasions on which it is necessary, but it is quite another to sneer ignorantly at non-standard varieties, or, worse still, to regard those who speak them as lazy, slovenly or even stupid.

One last point. It is possible that you have not been persuaded by my arguments in this chapter. Perhaps your temperature has been rising all the time you've been reading it, and perhaps you yourself are one of those people who consider it a moral duty to say *Whom did you see?* or to avoid splitting infinitives. If so, I am very sorry, but I have very good reasons for disagreeing with you. But please do not accuse me of claiming that 'any sort of English is equally good'. I am most emphatically *not* claiming anything of the sort. We are all familiar with examples of English speech and writing which are verbose, obscure and pretentious, or which are careless, slovenly, inexplicit and hard to follow. I am just as distressed as you are by such bad style, and I consider it a matter of importance to speak and write English with as much clarity, grace, vividness and explicitness as we can muster. I even laboriously correct my students' atrocious punctuation. But this is a completely separate issue from what I've been discussing in the chapter. Non-standard English can be wonderfully vivid and expressive, while many of the truly awful samples of English we run into are couched in impeccable standard English: legal and official documents, the turgid statements of politicians and military men, even some of the prose produced by my academic colleagues. If saying *whom* and avoiding split infinitives contributed anything to the quest for clarity and grace, I would be all for them, but they do nothing of the sort. Quite apart from being real English, split infinitives, sentence-final prepositions and our normal use of *hopefully* are almost always clearer and more elegant than any alternative, and those who rail against them, for whatever reason, are railing against good English style, and demanding instead something which is turgid and bad.

Language and identity: a reprise

In Chapter 4 we saw that an individual's way of speaking constitutes an important part of his or her identity within the community. This relation between language and identity also exists on a much larger scale, between entire languages and entire populations. The importance of this relation has been repeatedly underscored in the last two centuries by political events in dozens of countries. Let us briefly examine two of these cases.

We begin with Norwegian. Norway was for centuries a province of Denmark, and the official language of the country was, of course, Danish. All educated Norwegians knew Danish, and the Norwegian speech of the populous south of the country (just across the strait from Denmark) was heavily influenced by Danish. The remote villages of the west coast, in contrast, were little affected by

Danish, and, when Norway finally gained its independence in 1814, southern Norwegian was in many respects actually more similar to Danish than to the western dialects. (For example, southern Norwegian, like Danish, had only two grammatical genders, while western Norwegian had three.)

Upon independence, the Norwegians quickly agreed that Norwegian should replace Danish as the language of the country. There was nothing surprising about this. Every former colony which has gained its independence in this century has opted for a similar policy, and for the same reasons: we are no longer second-class Danes/Britons/Russians; we are a distinct people with our own nation and our own identity, and the most obvious outward sign of our identity is our language.

So everyone in Norway was agreed that Norwegian should be the language of the new nation. That sounds like a consensus, but a consensus there was not. The problem was this: *what sort* of Norwegian? Some Norwegians argued as follows: 'All educated people speak a form of Norwegian which is close to Danish. Let us therefore make this Dano-Norwegian our national language, because this will minimize the disruption involved in establishing the language.' Others, however, took a very different view: 'Dano-Norwegian is a corrupt form of Norwegian, little more than bad Danish. The *real* Norwegian is what they speak on the west coast, which has been little affected by Danish and which is the purest form of the language. This must therefore be our national language.'

This second position, of course, represents the kind of purism I discussed above, but it also represents another very common desire on the part of newly established national languages which have long been submerged by more powerful neighbours: the desire for **Abstand**. This German word means 'linguistic distance', and the point here is that the second group of Norwegians were anxious to distance their language from the closely related Danish, for fear that outsiders might continue to regard Norwegian as little more than an eccentric dialect of Danish.

In Norway, neither side in the debate succeeded in gaining the upper hand, with the result that Norway, a nation of 4 million people, wound up with *two* standard forms of Norwegian, with everybody obliged to learn both. This preposterous state of affairs has continued down to the present day, though the authorities are now making strenuous efforts to reach some sort of compromise on a single standard form. Just imagine the waste of time and money: everybody has to learn both forms in school, government documents have to be printed in both forms, and so on. Norway's story is a sobering reminder of just how deep linguistic passions can run.

My second case is the more contemporary one of Basque. Basque has been spoken for thousands of years at the western end of the Pyrenees, in territory which was once part of the Roman Empire and which was eventually incorporated into the nation-states of France and Spain, with the border running right through the Basque-speaking region. Throughout this time the language enjoyed little prestige. In the nineteenth and twentieth centuries, however, it began to be actively persecuted by centralist governments in Paris and Madrid which were increasingly inclined to see the use of regional languages as unpatriotic and subversive, an attitude which has been all too common among governments round the world in this century. This persecution reached its height on the Spanish side after the Fascist victory in the Spanish Civil War, when the Spanish dictator General Franco declared the very speaking of Basque to be illegal.

With the gradual easing of Franco's restrictions, and particularly after the democratic reforms that followed the old dictator's death, the Basques began to clamber for political rights, a struggle which finally culminated in the granting of autonomy to most Spanish Basques (the French Basques have not been so fortunate). And along with the political struggle, of course, there was a fight to improve the position of the Basque language.

Generations of neglect and persecution, combined with the exclusive use of Spanish (or French) for education, business, politics, administration, publishing and scholarship, had left Basque in a weakened state. Worse, the spread of the mass media had brought an insidious new threat: now even the most remote Basque farmhouse was bombarded with radio and television broadcasts in another language.

Like the Norwegians and many others before them, the Basques therefore set out to enhance the position of their language, with the goal of constructing a standard variety accessible to all Basques, and further of making Basque at least co-official with Spanish in the autonomous region. And, like the Norwegians before them, they faced some daunting obstacles, beginning with the obvious question: *what sort* of Basque should be promoted?

Though quite small, the Basque Country is criss-crossed by mountain ranges which chop the land up into narrow valleys, and the regional dialects of Basque differ from one another more greatly than do the dialects of English in England. Vocabulary, pronunciation, grammatical forms – all of these can change dramatically in the space of a few kilometres.

This state of affairs naturally called for an almost astronomical amount of decision-making and compromise. Most people were eager to see the creation of a single standard form of the language, but, at the same time, nobody wanted to abandon the particular words and forms he'd grown up with in favour of somebody else's usages. Moreover, the Basques, like everybody else, had their own views of other people's varieties. The Spanish Basques complained that the French Basques sounded patronizing and pretentious, while the French Basques complained in turn that the Spanish Basques sounded slovenly and crude. And everybody agreed that the speakers of the Bizkaian dialect were impossible to understand. Little by little, however, the highly regarded linguists of the Basque Language Academy put together the skeleton of a new standard form of Basque, called *Euskara Batua*, or Unified Basque (the Basques call their language *euskara*). Enthusiastically in some cases, grudgingly in others, the Basques have gradually accepted the new standard, so that today the majority of younger speakers can speak and write Batua as well as their local dialect.

Not that everything went smoothly. One of the strangest incidents in the whole political history of European languages traumatized the country throughout the 1970s: the War of the Aitches.

The French Basques have a consonant /h/, which they pronounce in many hundreds of words and which they have always written in their traditional spelling. Hence French Basques write, and pronounce, *hau* 'this', *horma* 'wall', *aho* 'mouth', *behar* 'need', *alhaba* 'daughter' and *ethorri* 'come'. The Spanish Basques lost all their aitches many centuries ago, long before Basque began to be written down, and the Spanish Basques write, and pronounce, *au*, *orma*, *ao*, *bear*, *alaba* and *etorri*. At least for purposes of writing, the Academy had to make a decision about this, and it adopted the delicate compromise of writing the *h* everywhere where the French Basques had it except after a consonant. Hence the Batua forms of these words are *hau*, *horma*, *aho*, *behar*, but *alaba*, *etorri*.

A good decision? Many outside observers thought so, but the result sent the Spanish Basques into convulsions. At a time of great political strain (this was the period when the dying Franco was using his police for one final, and murderous, attempt at stamping out Basque aspirations), these aitches brought about an unprecedented alliance between left-wing and right-wing Basques. The left-wingers objected bitterly to having *any* aitches in Batua, on the ground that silent consonants would make the written language more remote from the speech of the masses (conveniently overlooking the fact that standard Spanish does exactly the same thing: it writes hundreds of silent aitches). The right-wingers objected even more bitterly on the rather less subtle ground that they'd never had aitches before, and didn't see why they should have them now.

Any rational discussion about the development of Batua was all but drowned by the resulting furore. The right-wingers, who were mostly elderly and usually both very fluent and very literate in Basque, might have used their knowledge to influence that development in useful directions, but instead they expended their energies in writing newspaper articles, pamphlets and at least one entire book fulminating against Batua in general and aitches in particular. They sneered at the new standard as 'euskeranto' (a pun on the name of the famous artificial language Esperanto), and they hurled about such words as 'poison' and 'cancer', previously rarely seen in discussions of spelling systems. The left-wingers, who were typically less literate in Basque, contented themselves with angry speeches at mass meetings and the occasional diatribe in an underground magazine. A handful of linguists and other specialists continued to work quietly away on the essential business of creating tens of thousands of new words, to allow Basques to talk about such varied subjects as physics, economics, publishing and linguistics in their language (this entire process is called **language planning**), but, in the street, hardly anyone seemed to be talking about anything except aitches.

It passed, of course. The elderly right-wing opponents grew older and died, while the young left-wingers merely became middle-aged wage-earners with families, and for them jobs and children came to seem more important than aitches. Today, two decades later, everybody puts the aitches just where the Academy decided to put them all those years ago. I can't recall the last time I even heard somebody mention the subject of aitches. Forgotten though it is today, the War of the Aitches stands as testimony to the passions which can be evoked by even the most trivial linguistic issue. Language is different from other things.

Further reading

The remarks by Philip Howard on *hopefully* are taken from Howard (1977), but a good library will provide a number of books by Mr Howard and others expressing similar views about innovations in English. In fact, this particular outburst from Mr Howard is rather surprising, because elsewhere in the same book he argues forcefully for exactly the same general position as I have defended in this chapter. A readable and up-to-date summary of French efforts to stem the tide of English loans is given in Noreiko (1993). The tongue-in-cheek version of 'pure' English is taken from Jennings (1966). Some fascinating information on the enormous variation in English is provided in Trudgill (1990), Trudgill and Chambers (1991) and Milroy and Milroy (1993); the first chapter of the last book is a summary of attitudes to non-standard varieties. A discussion of language planning, including the Norwegian case, can be found in Chapter 5 of Holmes (1992).

Going further

I hope you have enjoyed this book enough to want to read more about language. I've already suggested some suitable further reading for the particular topics covered in my chapters; here are some more general works which you will find approachable and enjoyable.

Hudson (1984) is a very elementary introduction to the field of linguistics, including the techniques that linguists use in order to analyse language data. Aitchison (1992) is a slightly more detailed introduction, but still very readable. Fromkin and Rodman (1993) is a university-level textbook, but an outstandingly good one. Crystal (1987) is a well-illustrated encyclopedia providing fascinating information about almost every aspect of language.

If you'd like to read more about English in particular, Crystal (1988b) is a light-hearted but still substantial look at everything from Old English to truckers' slang, while both Bolton and Crystal (1993) and the much larger Gramley and Pätzold (1992) are

183

general surveys of the language.

Finally, Jackendoff (1993) and the much larger Pinker (1994) are both magnificent books which lay out the most important findings of modern linguistic science in an approachable and illuminating manner; anyone interested in language should read these books.

References

Aitchison, Jean. 1987. *Words in the Mind: An Introduction to the Mental Lexicon*. Oxford: Blackwell.

———1989. *The Articulate Mammal: An Introduction to Psycholinguistics*, 3rd edn. London: Routledge.

———1991. *Language Change: Progress or Decay?*, 2nd edn. Cambridge: Cambridge University Press.

———1992. *Teach Yourself Linguistics*, 4th edn. London: Hodder & Stoughton.

Barber, C. L. 1993. *The English Language: A Historical Introduction*. Cambridge: Cambridge University Press.

Bauer, Laurie. 1994. *Watching English Change*. London: Longman.

Baugh, Albert C. and Thomas Cable. 1993. *A History of the English Language*, 4th edn. London: Routledge.

Berlin, Brent and Paul Kay. 1969. *Basic Color Terms: Their Universality and Evolution*. Berkeley, CA: University of California Press.

Bickerton, Derek. 1981. *Roots of Language*. Ann Arbor, MI: Karoma.

———1990. *Language and Species*. Chicago: University of Chicago Press.

Bolton, W. F. and David Crystal (eds). 1993. *The Penguin History of Literature*, vol. 10: *The English Language*. London: Penguin.

Bonvillain, Nancy. 1993. *Language, Culture, and Communication: The Meaning of Messages*. Englewood Cliffs, NJ: Prentice-Hall.

Brown, Keith and Jim Miller. 1991. *Syntax: A Linguistic Introduction to Sentence Structure*, 2nd edn. London: HarperCollins.

Brown, Roger. 1973. *A First Language: The Early Stages*. London: George Allen & Unwin.

Chambers, J. K. and Peter Trudgill. 1980. *Dialectology*. Cambridge: Cambridge University Press.

Coates, Jennifer. 1993. *Women, Men and Language*, 2nd edn. London: Longman.

Comrie, Bernard. 1985. *Tense*. Cambridge: Cambridge University Press.

Corbett, Greville. 1991. *Gender*. Cambridge: Cambridge University Press.

Crowley, Terry. 1992. *An Introduction to Historical Linguistics*, 2nd edn. Oxford: Oxford University Press.

Cruse, David. 1986. *Lexical Semantics*. Cambridge: Cambridge University Press.

Crystal, David. 1987. *The Cambridge Encyclopedia of Language*. Cambridge: Cambridge University Press.

——1988a. *Rediscover Grammar*. London: Longman.

——1988b. *The English Language*. London: Penguin.

Curtiss, Susan. 1977. *Genie: A Psycholinguistic Study of a Modern-day 'Wild Child'*. New York: Academic Press.

Dixon, R. M. W. 1972. *The Dyirbal Language of North Queensland*. Cambridge: Cambridge University Press.

——1980. *The Languages of Australia*. Cambridge: Cambridge University Press.

Elliot, Alison J. 1981. *Child Language*. Cambridge: Cambridge University Press.

Fabb, Nigel. 1994. *Sentence Structure*. London: Routledge.

Francis, W. N. 1983. *Dialectology: An Introduction*. London: Longman.

Frawley, William. 1992. *Linguistic Semantics*. Hillsdale, NJ: Lawrence Erlbaum Associates.

Fromkin, Victoria A. 1973. *Speech Errors as Linguistic Evidence*. The Hague: Mouton.

——1980. *Errors in Linguistic Performance: Slips of the Tongue, Ear, Pen, and Hand*. New York: Academic Press.

Fromkin, Victoria and Robert Rodman. 1993. *An Introduction to Language*, 5th edn. Fort Worth, TX: Harcourt Brace Jovanovich.

Gazzaniga, Michael S. 1992. *Nature's Mind: The Biological Roots of Thinking, Emotions, Sexuality, Language and Intelligence*. New York: Basic Books.

Geschwind, Norman. 1979. 'Specializations of the human brain'. *Scientific American* 241 (September): 158–68.

Graddol, David and Joan Swann. 1989. *Gender Voices*. Oxford: Blackwell.

Gramley, Stephan and Kurt-Michael Pätzold. 1992. *A Survey of Modern English*. London: Routledge.

Haiman, John. 1980. *Hua: A Papuan Language of the Eastern Highlands of New Guinea*. Amsterdam: Benjamins.

Hawkins, John and Murray Gell-Mann (eds). 1992. *The Evolution of Human Languages*. Proceedings Volume XI, Santa Fe Institute. Redwood Park, CA: Addison-Wesley.

Hockett, Charles F. 1960. 'The origin of speech'. *Scientific American* 203: 88–96.

Hoffman, Th. R. 1993. *Realms of Meaning*. London: Longman.

Hofstadter, Douglas R. 1985. 'A person paper on purity in language'. In Douglas R. Hofstadter, *Metamagical Themas: Questing for the Essence of Mind and Pattern*, pp. 159–67. Harmondsworth: Viking Penguin.

Holmes, Janet. 1992. *An Introduction to Sociolinguistics*. London: Longman.

Howard, Philip. 1977. *New Words for Old*. London: Hamish Hamilton.

Hudson, Richard A. 1980. *Sociolinguistics*. Cambridge: Cambridge University Press.

——1984. *Invitation to Linguistics*. Oxford: Blackwell.

Hughes, Arthur and Peter Trudgill. 1979. *English Accents and Dialects*. London: Edward Arnold.

Hurford, James R. and Brendan Heasley. 1983. *Semantics: A Coursebook*. Cambridge: Cambridge University Press.

Ingram, Jay. 1992. *Talk Talk Talk*. Toronto: Penguin.

Jackendoff, Ray. 1993. *Patterns in the Mind: Language and Human Nature*. New York: Harvester Wheatsheaf.

Jackson, Howard. 1988. *Words and their Meaning*. London: Longman.

Jennings, Paul. 1966. '1066 and all Saxon', part 2. *Punch*, 22 June 1966, pp. 904–6.

Kramarae, C. 1981. *Women and Men Speaking: Frameworks for Analysis*. Rowley, MA: Newbury House.

Leakey, Richard. 1994. *The Origin of Humankind*. London: Weidenfeld & Nicolson.

Leech, Geoffrey. 1974. *Semantics*. Harmondsworth: Penguin.

Lehmann, Winfred P. 1992. *Historical Linguistics*, 3rd edn. London: Routledge.

Levinson, Stephen C. 1983. *Pragmatics*. Cambridge: Cambridge University Press.

Lieberman, Philip. 1975. *On the Origins of Language: An Introduction to the Evolution of Human Speech*. London: Macmillan.

——1984. *The Biology and Evolution of Language*. Cambridge, MA: Harvard University Press.

Linden, Eugene. 1974. *Apes, Men and Language*. Harmondsworth: Penguin.

Lockwood, W. B. 1969. *Indo-European Philology*. London: Hutchinson.

——1972. *A Panorama of Indo-European Languages*. London: Hutchinson.

Lyons, John. 1971. *An Introduction to Theoretical Linguistics*. Cambridge: Cambridge University Press.

Manser, Martin. 1988. *The Guinness Book of Words*. Enfield: Guinness Books.

McCrum, Robert, William Cran and Robert MacNeil. 1992. *The Story of English*. London: Faber & Faber/BBC Books.

McMahon, April M. S. 1994. *Understanding Language Change*. Cambridge: Cambridge University Press.

Mey, Jacob L. 1993. *Pragmatics*. Oxford: Blackwell.

Miller, Casey and Kate Swift. 1980. *The Handbook of Nonsexist Writing*. New York: Barnes & Noble.

Milroy, James. 1992. *Linguistic Variation and Change*. Oxford: Blackwell.

Milroy, James and Lesley Milroy (eds). 1993. *Real English: The Grammar of English Dialects in the British Isles*. London: Longman.

Motley, Michael T. 1985. 'Slips of the tongue'. *Scientific American* 253 (September): 114–19.

Motluk, Alison. 1994. 'The sweet smell of purple'. *New Scientist* 1938 (13 August): 32–7.

Noreiko, Stephen. 1993. 'New words for new technologies'. In Carol Sanders (ed.), *French Today*, pp. 171–84. Cambridge: Cambridge University Press.

Palmer, Frank. 1984. *Grammar*, 2nd edn. Harmondsworth: Penguin.

Peccei, Jean Stilwell. 1994. *Child Language*. London: Routledge.

Pinker, Steven. 1994. *The Language Instinct: The New Science of Language and Mind*. London: Allen Lane/Penguin.

Platt, John, Heidi Weber and Ho Min Lian. 1984. *The New Englishes*. London: Routledge.

Pullum, Geoffrey K. 1991. *The Great Eskimo Vocabulary Hoax and Other*

Irreverent Essays on the Study of Language. Chicago: University of Chicago Press.

Pyles, Thomas. 1971. *The Origin and Development of the English Language.* New York: Harcourt, Brace & World.

Romaine, Suzanne. 1994. *Language in Society: An Introduction to Sociolinguistics.* Oxford: Oxford University Press.

Rymer, Russ. 1993. *Genie: An Abused Child's Flight from Silence.* New York: HarperCollins. Expanded edition published 1994 as *Genie: A Scientific Tragedy,* London: Penguin.

Sacks, Oliver. 1985. *The Man Who Mistook His Wife for a Hat.* London: Duckworth.

Savage-Rumbaugh, E. Sue. 1986. *Ape Language: From Conditioned Response to Symbol.* New York: Columbia University Press.

Sebeok, Thomas A. and Jean Umiker-Sebeok (eds). 1980. *Speaking of Apes: A Critical Anthology of Two-Way Communication with Man.* New York: Plenum Press.

Sheard, J. A. 1966. *The Words of English.* New York: W. W. Norton.

Smith, Neil. 1989. *The Twitter Machine: Reflections on Language.* Oxford: Blackwell.

Spender, Dale. 1985. *Man Made Language.* London: Routledge & Kegan Paul.

Steinberg, Danny D. 1993. *An Introduction to Psycholinguistics.* London: Longman.

Strang, Barbara. 1970. *A History of English.* London: Methuen.

Trask, R. L. 1994. *Language Change.* London: Routledge.

Trudgill, Peter. 1974. *Sociolinguistics.* Harmondsworth: Penguin.

———1990. *The Dialects of England.* Oxford: Blackwell.

———1994. *Dialects.* London: Routledge.

Trudgill, Peter and J. K. Chambers (eds). 1991. *Dialects of English: Studies in Grammatical Variation.* London: Longman.

Trudgill, Peter and Jean Hannah. 1994. *International English: A Guide to the Varieties of Standard English,* 3rd edn. London: Edward Arnold.

Wallman, Joel. 1992. *Aping Language.* Cambridge: Cambridge University Press.

Wells, John C. 1982. *Accents of English,* 3 volumes. Cambridge: Cambridge University Press.

Whorf, Benjamin Lee. 1956. *Language, Thought and Reality: Selected Writings of Benjamin Lee Whorf,* edited by J. B. Carroll. New York: MIT Press.

Williams, Joseph M. 1975. *Origins of the English Language: A Social and Linguistic History.* London: Collier Macmillan.

Index